# POSITIVE POLITICS

# POSITIVE POLITICS

★

## A PROVEN PLAYBOOK TO GET INTO POLITICS, CHANGE YOUR LIFE, AND CHANGE THE WORLD

NEIL THANEDAR

**LIONCREST**
PUBLISHING

POSITIVE POLITICS
*A Proven Playbook to Get into Politics, Change Your Life, and Change the World*

FIRST EDITION

ISBN   978-1-5445-5047-3   *Hardcover*
       978-1-5445-5046-6   *Paperback*
       978-1-5445-5048-0   *Ebook*

*To Kai, Ajay, and Maya, who teach me how to be a better father, friend, and leader every day.*

*What is a leader?*

*"A leader helps people."*

*—Kai Thanedar, age six*

# CONTENTS

# PART II: HOW

# INTRODUCTION

It's 1992 in a small, faded-yellow split-level home in south St. Louis. Nothing about this place says "future president lives here"—except for the man inside, who's sitting on the ground in front of an old box TV with his four-year-old son, watching Bill Clinton accept the Democratic nomination for president. "That could be you!" he tells the boy.

Twenty-four years later, around a big kitchen table in south Ann Arbor, watching the news about the 2016 presidential results and the upcoming gubernatorial election in Michigan, I get to return the message. "That could be you!" I tell my dad.

Shri Thanedar wasn't supposed to get out of his village in India, let alone all the way to the Michigan State Capitol and US Congress. He worked his way out of poverty, working nights, graduating college early at eighteen, and getting a master's degree in Bombay before coming to America in 1979 to get his PhD. Shri became a US citizen in 1988 and quit his research job to start his first business in 1990. For ten years, he bootstrapped his lab from under $100,000 per year to over $3 million in annual revenue and then got bank financing to acquire nine other labs around the country and grow them to over $50 million in annual revenue.

Then in 2008, just when he started getting offers to sell his company for over $100 million, the economy crashed, his business had two bad quarters, and Bank of America took over, rushing to sell his businesses and our home, cars, and more for far below their real value so the bank could get its money back quickly. The bank got 100 percent of its money (plus interest), while we were left with less than 1 percent of what we previously had.

I was a junior and senior at the University of Michigan at the time, and I remember getting lots of calls from Dad. I would pace the hallways outside the school library, and we would talk for hours about what to do next. Those ideas turned into Avomeen. Our startup, which began as just the two of us in an old lab in Ann Arbor, sold for over $30 million just six years later in 2016, and now employs about one hundred Michiganders.

Dad retired at the age of sixty-one—for a few months. He traveled to South America for the first time. He took an extended trip to Europe. It was relaxing, but he quickly got bored. By Christmas 2016, he was itching to do something new. Would it be another lab? Maybe an investment firm? Should we create a startup accelerator together? But nothing that was focused on making more money seemed satisfying to him.

In one conversation, Dad said, "If my health is good, I have twenty good years left. What's the best way to use this time?" We looked up at the TV on the wall, playing CNN's political coverage, and the tension was obvious. We all knew the problems, but who was working on the solutions? We didn't know any politicians whom we could call and convince to change any policies, let alone politics as a whole. What should we do?

"You should run for governor of Michigan. It's an open seat in 2018. The last governor failed. There's a huge opportunity here," I said. There was a long list of establishment candidates rumored to be running on both sides, but no one stood out yet.

Dad protested. "I can't run for governor! I have an accent. Will people in rural Michigan really vote for me?"

"You have everything you need to win. A great story, great experience, and the time and money you need to talk to the whole state. Let's do it!"

While my dad earned over 200,000 votes and won the city of Detroit, he lost that first election in 2018. But he immediately ran again for state representative in 2020 and won, then ran for US Congress in 2022 and 2024 and won again both times. As Detroit's congressman and member of the Homeland Security, Small Business, and Agriculture committees, he has introduced bills to fight discrimination by the TSA and ICE, improve access to mental health support for all, and make competing for government contracts easier for startups. It's clear to see, and he agrees—this past decade has easily been the most meaningful and impactful of his life.

### WANT TO MAKE A BIGGER IMPACT BUT DON'T KNOW WHERE TO START?

Does it feel like the world is falling apart and there's nothing you can do to fix it? Are you frustrated by the current negativity and cynicism in politics, especially online? Does it feel like the worst people are in charge of our government and our best people are on the sidelines? Do you want to be more politically active and make the world a better place but don't know where to start?

These feelings are surprisingly common throughout history. If you had been born just over one hundred years ago as part of the Greatest Generation, with a childhood defined by the Great Depression, the answer of what to do would be obvious: fight, in the war or on the home front, and do whatever you could do to save the world. But where are the front lines now?

The fight for our future is now in politics. Congress still holds the sole power to declare war. But the decisions made daily on fundamental issues like education, healthcare, jobs, and housing can do even more to shape our world for future generations. And most of these decisions are not made in Washington, DC. They're made at your state capitol, or your city council, or your local school board. You have many paths to making a positive political impact, starting with local activism.

The sneaky secret of politics is that the people on the inside want it to look complicated so you'll leave it to them. When you see politics on TV, you're seeing the perfectly polished version of what they want you to see. But I've been backstage with the president, next to the speechwriters, reading the teleprompters. These are all just real people: stressed, tired, and doing their best to keep the country running. You are absolutely capable of being one of these people. You have the skills; you have the drive; you have the vision. You just need to get started.

To be a great politician, you don't need to be a rich, famous genius with friends in high places. You don't need to belong to a specific party or be a specific age. But you do need some special qualities. Most importantly, you must be an ambitious optimist. Ambition by itself is often wasted by those who cynically chase money. But the rare people who pair their ambition with an eternal optimism that problems can always be solved frequently succeed in politics. Think Theodore Roosevelt's "Man in the Arena" or Margaret Mead's "small group of thoughtful, committed citizens" who change the world. These are ambitious optimists.

## WHO IS AN AMBITIOUS OPTIMIST?

Startup founders are often ambitious optimists, because it takes a relentless drive toward a positive vision for the future to turn big ideas into reality. But ambitious optimism can be much broader, from people already working in public service for nonprofits and government agencies to authors, artists, and activists mobilizing the public to act. Does solving problems energize you? Are you always looking for ways for you to positively change the world? Then you're an ambitious optimist!

Ambitious optimists are energized by solving problems and are always looking for ways to positively change the world.

In our country's darkest moments, we remember FDR's words that "the only thing we have to fear is fear itself" or JFK's encouragement to "Ask not what your country can do for you—ask what you can do for your country." From the Declaration of Independence to Lincoln's Gettysburg Address through Martin Luther King Jr.'s "I Have a Dream" speech, the idea that "this nation will rise up and live out the true meaning of its creed... that all men are created equal" is fundamentally an ambitious optimist's vision in times of crisis. We need that energy again.

Don't know how to get started? This book will help. But first I want you to think through all the reasons why you haven't started already. Are you scared of getting into politics because you might get personally attacked? Do you think politics is impossible to fix? Are you waiting until you're rich and famous to have a bigger impact in politics?

## I'M HERE TO HELP YOU OVERCOME THESE FEARS THROUGH ACTION

Inaction is scary too. What happens if you never get into politics? Will you feel stuck on the hamster wheel of making money? What if you never leave a lasting positive impact on the world? Will you live a life that makes your kids proud? Don't defer happiness until retirement. Go do that big scary ambitious thing now. Find your highest calling and commit the rest of your life to it. Are you looking for a better way to channel your ambitious optimism into positive action and impact? Then politics is for you.

This book introduces six simple principles that make Positive Politics easy to follow. They come in three pairs, to remind you of the required trade-offs. First, be nice *and* take action. Focus on issues over attacks and do the work to solve those issues. Second, get wins quickly *and* think long term. While early success builds momentum, ultimate success is measured over decades. Third, go direct *and* be independent. Use modern media to reach the public directly and lessen the power of money over you. By following these Positive Politics principles, detailed in Chapter 1, you'll set yourself up to win elections and do good for decades.

## WHY POSITIVE POLITICS?

When you think "politics," is the first image in your head two people arguing on cable news? That's politics at its worst: a popularity contest focused on trying to win fifteen minutes of fame each day. Tomorrow, the breaking news will be different, and the same group of negative politicians will scramble to chase that story. This negative politics gets a lot of attention now.

Positive Politics is a better way for ambitious optimists to take political action, win elections, and change the world. Politics is at its best when we zoom out and focus on positively shaping our long-term future. If we all work together, what can we improve in a year? A decade? A lifetime? By focusing on these fundamentals, we will be more successful politically and our society will be happier and stronger.

This book seeks to build the knowledge and confidence you need to get into politics—and do good. You'll learn of the many different paths that political leaders have taken to success, with a particular focus on their first steps into the field. From passing your first bill as an activist to winning your first race as a politician, you'll also learn how new trends and platforms are changing which strategies will work best for you. These strategies have worked for members of all parties, from antiquity to the modern era, in countries around the world.

This book also addresses common fears that keep people out of politics. The fear of failure and the idea of being a public figure scare too many of our best people away from politics. And the specters of cynicism and corruption make it hard to get started. But ambitious optimists like you are exactly who we need in our politics now. If you want to experience more meaning in your life and make a bigger impact on the world, Positive Politics is for you. This book will show you exactly how to get started in politics and quickly do good.

Once you start getting stuff done in politics, you'll see opportunities to make positive changes everywhere. From taking action on your first issue as an individual activist to organizing collective action to make lasting political changes, this book explains how to get into politics, change your life, and change the world. The sum of all of this work is Positive Politics.

**WHAT THIS BOOK WILL TEACH YOU**

This book has ten core chapters, split into two parts—"Why" and "How":

1. **Why Positive?** Negativity is winning now. But the pendulum's always swinging in politics. By focusing on issues over attacks, we can help spark the next positive era.
2. **Why Politics?** Politics and government are two of the most powerful tools to change the world. Get into politics now and use this power for good.
3. **Why Now?** Stop waiting for the world to change and do the work to fix it. We will be the ones to turn society from the current crisis to our next awakening.
4. **Why You?** We tend to put activists and politicians on a pedestal, but even famous historical figures started simply. You can get into politics quickly too, and this will positively change your life and the world.
5. **Why Fight?** Others are using negativity to win now. Positivity doesn't just happen. We have to fight for it. Let's be happy warriors fighting for the Good Future.
6. **How to Get Started:** The best way to get into politics is to start with activism. This will teach you skills like how to write and pass bills, how to work with politicians of all parties, and how to rally attention and money for your mission.

7. **How to Get Stuff Done:** Activism isn't just about protesting. It's about getting politicians to change laws and solve problems. Here's a simple playbook for individual and group activism that you can use to make political change now.

8. **How to Build Power:** The greatest activist movements all relied on collective action, mobilizing armies of support. Think about the millions marching with Gandhi and MLK. Here's how to earn political capital and organize support to solve problems.

9. **How to Win Elections:** Politics isn't easy, but it is simple. All you have to do is earn one more vote than the next-best candidate. Here's how to pick the right race and win.

10. **How to Change the World:** Now that you're equipped with the tools to succeed in activism and politics, use this power to change the world through Positive Politics.

I've also included a special eleventh chapter, "What's Next?" Too many political books are heavy on theory and light on action. The first part of this chapter, section 11.1, explains my plan to recruit more ambitious optimists into politics, and section 11.2 includes my top-ten list of big issues to inspire you to take action. Committing your next career to solving these problems through politics will change your life and change the world.

## WHY I'M WRITING THIS BOOK

For the first decade of my part-time political career, I was still focused on my second startup, Labdoor, all day, getting home by 6:00 or 7:00 p.m. and then immediately getting on the phone for an hour or two or three of political strategizing with Dad. I thought that I could have it all—startup, politics, family—but I wasn't really doing any of the three to my full potential. I kept promising myself that I'd go all in on politics once I sold this business, but I also didn't want to force a sale. Three serious acquisition offers fell through in those five years, the last after a process lasting more than six months, during which we built the business to run without me.

After that third almost-exit, I took time off to decide what to do next. I started a nonprofit during COVID-19. I made a series of angel investments that were successful enough (including a $10,000 investment that returned $200,000) that I seriously considered investing full time. I also co-founded a third startup and helped this company sprint to more than $10 million raised in less than a year. I was solving problems. But were they really the biggest problems?

Then something amazing happened. I found out I was having my third kid—my first girl. Baby Maya was born on December 11, 2024, and I decided to take my first ever real paternity leave. This time, I decided that my focus must be family first, politics second, and everything else last. I have ten years until my oldest goes to college and less than twenty years of my kids' childhoods left. Life's too short to focus on anything else.

So I started writing this book. And through the process of learning and sharing the stories of many great activists turned politicians, I realized that I could be doing so much more political work now. I found an opportunity to lead a nonprofit fighting dark money in Michigan politics, I applied, and two months later I was unanimously elected by the board to lead the Michigan Campaign Finance Network. MCFN is now my home for political and activism work, and I've already been able to chase and break multiple investigations into corruption and waste in Michigan politics.

After a decade of part-time politics, making politics my career has made me feel like I'm starting a whole new life. It's so invigorating to wake up every morning and get to fight what I think is the number one problem in politics—corruption. By sharing my story and those of so many others through this book, I hope to inspire the current generation of ambitious optimists to get into politics now. I want to make Positive Politics into a movement, with hundreds of new leaders positively impacting millions or even billions of people. This is the most meaningful and impactful work we could be doing now. I love this feeling of truly living my dream life now!

I'm writing this book to inspire more ambitious people to work on the world's biggest problems. So much of the world's top talent is being wasted chasing money, and so much of our politics is controlled by a small group of elites and special interests. Positive Politics is a meta-solution to these big problems. Ambitious optimists like you have the skills and experience needed to succeed in activism and politics. This book explains why and how anyone can get into politics positively and win. I'll explain how to do this starting in Chapter 6.

## WHAT THIS BOOK IS AND ISN'T

This book is for any ambitious optimist looking to positively change the world. If you have the passion, vision, and determination to focus on a mission for a decade or more and keep getting stuff done despite negative opposition, then *Positive Politics* is for you.

This book isn't for cynics, critics, and complainers. Cable news and social media are already doing enough for these people. This book also isn't for people motivated by fame and power. They should read *The 48 Laws of Power* or *The Prince*.

Positive Politics is a long game—this isn't a shortcut to success. And this book is not for those who see politics as a way to get rich. Positively changing the world through activism is a rewarding life, but it doesn't pay well.

This book isn't for partisans. Positive Politics requires actions that don't neatly fit into any one party. While most of my personal experience comes from Democratic politics, these Positive Politics strategies work for Republicans and independents too. I know because I've helped my friends from across the political spectrum find their lanes and start with activism. Positive Politics is about rising above partisanship and fighting for the fundamentals for all Americans.

I'm writing this book to launch the Positive Politics movement. We need our own Positive Politics community, events, and media to organize our efforts and energies. Most importantly, we need more ambitious optimists like you in our politics. Every person who joins our community grows our movement's power and potential. That's why I've created this actionable playbook that anyone can use to get into politics and do good.

**POSITIVE POLITICS IS SIMPLE**

1. Do the work.
2. Spread the word.

That's it. Start by taking one political action and see how it changes you. Share your success with your friends and family and see how it changes them. The greatest movements don't just change the world—they change the people in it. Get inspired to find new meaning and purpose through political action. Make politics your career and see how much bigger your life can be.

Positive Politics empowers us all to find where we can make the most impact now and get to work. We all have the power to make these changes as activists and politicians. This new Positive Politics movement is for everyone—young and old, rich and poor, left, right, and center. The only qualification is an earnest desire to positively change your world. If this excites you, keep reading—this book is for you!

# PART I

★

# WHY

# CHAPTER 1

\* \* \*

# WHY POSITIVE?

# 1.1

☆

# IT'S NOT PERSONAL

*"I will never attend an anti-war rally; if you have a peace rally, invite me."*

—MOTHER TERESA

On November 14, 1995, the two most powerful men in Washington, DC, were playing a $400 million game of chicken. Angry about being ignored by President Bill Clinton on a long trip to Prime Minister Yitzhak Rabin's funeral in Israel, Republican House Speaker Newt Gingrich passed a federal budget with major cuts to Medicare, Medicaid, and education spending that he knew Clinton would quickly veto. This caused a government shutdown, resulting in 800,000 federal employees, including 80 percent of the White House's paid staff, being furloughed.[1]

In his televised press conference that day, Clinton blamed Gingrich and congressional Republicans for putting America in this position, saying, "I strongly believe their budget plan is bad for America. I believe it will undermine opportunity...and make our country more divided." Polling at the time showed that the public blamed Gingrich more than Clinton for this shutdown.[2] But Clinton's victory was short-lived. The next evening, inside a White House where unpaid interns were brought in to cover for employees who had been furloughed, Clinton began an affair with one of these interns, twenty-two-year-old Monica Lewinsky.[3]

Gingrich succeeded in impeaching Bill Clinton on December 19, 1998, for lying under oath and obstructing justice in connection with this affair. During the height of this controversy, Gingrich called Clinton's affair "the most systematic, deliberate obstruction-of-justice cover-up and effort to avoid the truth we have ever seen in American history!"[4] But Gingrich's victory was also short-lived. That impeachment vote was Gingrich's last in the House. On January 3, 1999, Gingrich resigned from Congress after getting caught up in his own affair and ethics violation.

This public Gingrich versus Clinton battle of the 1990s sparked a decades-long era of divisive national politics. Three times as many Republicans and Democrats now have a "very unfavorable" view of the opposing party compared to thirty years ago.[5]

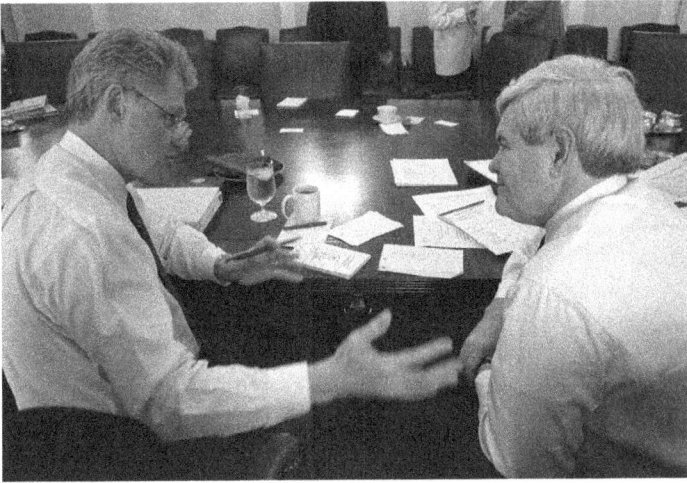

President Clinton and Speaker Gingrich in the 1995 Congressional budget negotiations.
Source: Robert McNeely, National Archives, 1995[6]

But the Clinton versus Gingrich rivalry was largely fake. Both leaders quietly worked together on reforming Social Security and Medicare and had plans to announce a bipartisan deal in Clinton's second term. After months of private negotiations between their closest aides, Clinton and Gingrich even met secretly at the White House on October 28, 1997, to finalize the US government's 1998 budget together.[7] However, this deal fell apart in January 1998 when the Clinton–Lewinsky scandal broke publicly and it was advantageous for Gingrich to personally attack Clinton again. Because of negative politics, numerous reforms that would have strengthened the social safety net and reduced the federal debt were never completed.

Negative politics also tends to breed hypocrisy. Despite his constant "family values" attacks, Gingrich was having his own affair with a House staffer while he led Clinton's impeachment in 1998. They were more alike personally and politically than either could admit.

Read *The Pact* by Steven M. Gillon to learn how Clinton's and Gingrich's similar origin stories led them to both their public successes and private failures.

## OUR POLITICS IS AT ITS WORST WHEN WE GET PERSONAL AND NEGATIVE

When our politics gets personal, real people suffer. The negativity in the Clinton versus Gingrich rivalry wasn't just a battle between two men. Hundreds of thousands of jobs and medical benefits for millions of Americans got stuck in the middle. Similarly, the partisan fight over healthcare reform starting in 2009—with the personalization of "Obamacare" and the fear around "death panels"—was another negative turning point in American politics. Fundamental issues like healthcare and jobs should not be overlooked because of personal disputes.

Our third negative turning point in modern American politics occurred in 2015. Donald Trump brought back the constantly combative style of his advisor Newt Gingrich, this time against Hillary Clinton. Since then, the incumbent party has lost three straight presidential elections. With public trust in government near historic lows, at 22 percent of Americans, including 35 percent of Democrats and 11 percent of Republicans, sticking to the status quo is a losing strategy.[8] Meanwhile, incumbents in both parties continue to escalate their attacks on each other.

The hidden cost of this negativity is the erosion of our political talent pool. Many potential leaders choose not to run for office because they don't want to subject themselves and their families to personal attacks. At the same time, Machiavellian, narcissistic politicians keep running and are rewarded with more attention and success. The result is a political class selected not for the ability to solve problems, but for skill at personal attacks.

## WHY NEGATIVITY IS WINNING

*"If everybody always lies to you, the consequence is not that you believe the lies, but rather that nobody believes anything any longer... And a people that no longer can believe anything cannot make up its mind. It is deprived not only of its capacity to act but also of its capacity to think and to judge. And with such a people you can then do what you please."*

—HANNAH ARENDT, 1973

I often get asked, "If Positive Politics is so great, why are so many negative politicians winning?" One reason is cyclical. The pendulum is always swinging in politics. As I'll explain in section 3.2, at least three different trends are currently shifting from negative to positive. But that's not enough for Positive Politics to win now and in the future. Negativity gets attention, like a toddler crying at the dinner table. Like strong parents, we must be calm, consistent, and confident in our plan to counter this negativity.

## HERE'S WHY NEGATIVITY WORKS

1. Negative politicians succeed in the short term by "flooding the zone" with lies.
2. As Arendt would say, these repeated lies lead to cynicism.
3. Cynicism creates an environment ripe for corruption.

**Negative Political Cycle**

Lies → Cynicism → Corruption

In politics, the positive cycle is simple too. You can't fight fire with fire. You need an extinguisher. The truth is a powerful extinguisher. But what we really need is a flood of transparency to wash away the cynicism and corruption. Fighting negativity is a never-ending job. But the positive cycle builds momentum with each revolution.

**Positive Political Cycle**

Transparency → Truth → Trust

The solution to one hundred messy lies is one simple truth repeated a hundred times. This is the positive path out of our current political civil war. So what's the one simple truth that all Positive Politicians should communicate? We can all fight for transparency. Good governance issues like campaign finance reform and open public contracts accelerate positive cycles. This empowers politicians, journalists, and citizens to follow the money, expose corruption, and do positive-sum work!

## HOW TO COUNTER NEGATIVITY

*"A lie can travel halfway around the world while the truth is putting on its shoes."*

—MARK TWAIN

The truth is that negativity works, especially in the short term. Combating lies is exhausting because it's like playing a never-ending game of Whac-A-Mole—and negative politicians want us to get stuck focusing on their lies. It's better to go straight to the truth and keep repeating it until the public listens.

**HERE ARE THREE WAYS TO USE POSITIVE POLITICS TO FIGHT NEGATIVITY**

1. **Start early.** Define yourself positively before opponents can attack you.
   - Example: Ukrainian President Volodymyr Zelenskyy, who has a law degree but became a comedian and actor and created his own production company in his first career, produced and starred in the TV series *Servant of the People*. In the series, he portrayed a teacher whose anticorruption rant goes viral, which leads to him becoming Ukrainian president. He later used *Servant of the People* as the name of his political party and became the anticorruption candidate and president that Ukrainians already knew and loved. Positive Politics works all over the world!
2. **Deflect negativity.** Use humor to stop attacks and focus on the issues.
   - Example: Michigan Governor Gretchen Whitmer learned from her political mentors to counter negativity with humor. She shared this advice: "Don't get mad at what they say; just say, 'Oh, come on. I know you don't believe that.'"[9] This was a valuable tactic for Whitmer as she served fourteen years in the Michigan House and Senate, all in the minority party, before becoming governor. As we discussed at the beginning of this chapter, political outrage is usually performative. Laugh it off and get back to the issues.

3. **Be relentlessly positive.** Unify people with a shared mission and get stuff done.
   ○ Example: Former California Governor Arnold Schwarzenegger is a prototypical ambitious optimist. He persevered for decades to succeed in three different careers, as a bodybuilder, actor, and politician, and is still working as an activist fighting for pro-environment and antigerrymandering reform. In his second inaugural address, he asked, "How can we grow into something greater, something better, something more meaningful without a dream to guide us?"[10] Schwarzenegger's relentless optimism can be an inspiration to anyone regardless of politics.

## WHY POSITIVITY IS MAKING A COMEBACK

"The angriest voices in Congress are mostly faking," according to former US Representative Jeff Jackson (D-NC), who earned millions of followers in his first term through direct and transparent messages and videos detailing what really happens in Congress.[11] He has publicly called out politicians who fake anger for media attention, saying, "The same people who act like maniacs during the open meetings are suddenly calm and rational during the closed ones. Why? Because there aren't any cameras in the closed meetings, so the incentives are different."

Being real, open, honest, and positive is the future of American politics. As Representative Jackson wrote in a blog post, "What I love about writing these updates—about communicating with you directly—is that the incentives can be different. They can be positive."[12]

The previous generation of politicians chose negative partisanship because it earned them TV coverage and fundraising dollars. Negativity works in short media segments, but it quickly burns people out. If we want politics to operate differently, we need to prove that we can direct attention and money to Positive Politicians who deliver the good results we need. This requires us to define our movement, recruit new leaders, take positive action, and build political power.

Both old and new media will be key to the Positive Politics movement. Direct long-form media, from books like this one to podcasts, online videos, and email newsletters, reward positivity because they help us build long-term relationships with our audiences. We need to learn how to bring more positivity to new short media formats, like TikTok and other platforms yet to be invented. The fundamentals of positivity, from defining yourself to focusing on a shared mission, can work on any media platform.

We also need to leverage the power of live events and rallies to energize our supporters and highlight our successes. What would a modern March on Washington or Montgomery bus boycott look like today? These protests positively focused our dreams, our rights, and our actions. Let's organize the positive rallies of our modern era!

## POSITIVITY IS DEFINED BY WHAT WE'RE FOR, NOT WHAT WE'RE AGAINST

Imagine political debates focused on policy instead of partisanship. And congressional hearings focused on celebrating positive government service instead of made-for-TV shouting matches. This is possible when Positive Politicians start early, focus on the truth, deflect negativity, and stay relentlessly positive. Why does this work so well? It has a lot to do with the game theory behind the prisoner's dilemma, which we'll look at next.

# 1.2

☆

# BEING NICE IS A WINNING STRATEGY

## THE PRISONER'S DILEMMA IN POLITICS

*Two members of a criminal gang are arrested and taken to separate rooms. The police tell the criminals that if they both stay silent, they will each get one year in jail. However, if just one criminal defects against the other, then the defector will go free and the other will get three years in jail. And if both criminals defect, they both will get two years in jail. What would you do?*

This puzzle is called the prisoner's dilemma, and it's actually a solved problem. Starting in 1977, University of Michigan political scientist Robert Axelrod created an annual series of prisoner's dilemma tournaments to test hundreds of different strategies submitted by researchers from around the world.

One strategy won multiple tournaments, even when the other players knew that same strategy would be repeated.[13]

## THE GAME THEORY OF A PRISONER'S DILEMMA IS SIMPLE

- Each player can choose to cooperate or defect.
- The best overall outcome is for everyone to cooperate.
- But individual players can get a better payoff if they defect.
- This incentivizes everyone to defect, *especially in low-trust environments.*

The number one winning strategy in Axelrod's prisoner's dilemma tournaments was called "Tit for Two Tats." Basically, you always cooperate first (be nice). Then you cooperate again (be forgiving). Then, only if the other player has defected twice, you defect once (be provokable). Then go back to cooperating (be predictable). If you always stick to these four rules, you will win the most in the long term, and the players who work with you will win more too.

## AXELROD'S FOUR RULES FOR SUCCESSFUL COOPERATION

1. **Be nice:** Always cooperate first.
2. **Be forgiving:** Give the other player two chances to cooperate.
3. **Be provokable:** Only punish once after being hurt twice. Then be nice again.
4. **Be predictable:** Always follow rules 1, 2, and 3 so other players know how to cooperate with you early.

One key to Axelrod's tournaments is that the players played many rounds together. In a single prisoner's dilemma, where real prison time is on the line and the two prisoners will never meet again, you might see why they would both defect. Mathematician John Nash won the 1994 Nobel Prize in Economics for introducing and analyzing the idea of cooperative versus noncooperative games and found that while games like the prisoner's dilemma can be noncooperative when played once, they are cooperative when played iteratively.[14] This distinction tells us to focus on the iterative nature of politics if we want to encourage long-term cooperation. Following Axelrod's four rules will make us all win more often in politics.

Politics is one big prisoner's dilemma. In the long term, the best option is for all of us to cooperate and be positive. But any one candidate can increase their short-term chances of winning once by going negative. In low-trust environments like partisan politics, this incentivizes everyone to defect and attack other candidates.

## AXELROD ENCOURAGES US TO USE POSITIVE-SUM THINKING

*"It's important to avoid words like 'opponent' and 'trying to defeat the other guy,' because that evokes zero-sum thinking. And this is not a zero-sum game. We all tend to fall into zero-sum thinking whenever there's any kind of rivalry or anything that looks like competition because zero-sum thinking is the easiest way to do it. And it's wrong and self-defeating in many contexts—in fact, almost all contexts except say sports and all-out war."*

—ROBERT AXELROD

It's easy to think of politics as a zero-sum game. In every race, one candidate wins, and the rest lose. But if we truly build a political movement full of positive candidates, we're not fighting against each other; we're actually working together to solve our country's biggest problems. This is especially true once we're in government. We should avoid the partisan battles that force zero-sum thinking and look to find common ground with anyone willing to work on important Positive Politics solutions with us.

Read *The Evolution of Cooperation* by Robert Axelrod to learn more about how specific actions and environments can foster cooperation.

## BUILD TRUST BEFORE THE GAME STARTS

Mafias build a culture where loyalty and cooperation are rewarded and double-crossing and defection are punished. Political parties operate very similarly. The result can be bad when this system is used to create fear and force corruption. But building trust before you start running for politics and making connections in all parties and factions once you're in government is the most effective long-term strategy for getting positive things done in politics.

In the 1980s, Republican President Ronald Reagan and Democratic Speaker of the House Tip O'Neill got so close that O'Neill was among the first people Reagan allowed to visit him in the hospital after the 1981 assassination attempt on his life. O'Neill got on his knees, prayed the 23rd Psalm, and then kissed Reagan on the forehead.[15] In the years that followed, they agreed to disagree during work hours, but "after 6:00 p.m."

they met as friends. We need to build more of these strong friendships across political parties.

In the 2008 presidential race, Barack Obama and John McCain mutually pledged to run positive, issues-focused campaigns. The two men had worked together in the US Senate and, like Reagan and O'Neill before them, disagreed politically but respected each other personally. They debated vigorously on the issues but also defended each other from personal attacks, like the time McCain countered the fear and conspiracy theories about Obama's citizenship by stopping a campaign event to explain "he's a decent family man, citizen, who I just happen to disagree with on fundamental issues."[16] Trust and respect are earned over time. Politics is a long, positive game when played correctly.

## POSITIVE POLITICS WAVES A BIG "COOPERATE" FLAG

Our flag isn't red or blue; it doesn't play into partisan divisions. The Positive Politics banner is *yellow*, for optimism, for the future. And there is strength in numbers. Every person who proudly labels themselves a Positive Politician and consistently follows their words with positive action signals to their opponents and to voters that there's a better way to win.

Game theory is all about signaling. If you can signal positivity early and often and back it up, you will win long-term iterated games like politics, even if negative opponents exploit your niceness in the short term. And remember that Axelrod didn't say you should cooperate every time. Give others two chances to cooperate, punish once after being exploited twice, then return to cooperating. This is the long-term winning strategy in activism and politics.

## THE SIX KEY PRINCIPLES AT THE CORE OF POSITIVE POLITICS

These principles come in three pairs, purposely designed to compete with each other. They might seem simple, but doing all of these things consistently is the difficult and valuable part.

1.  **Be nice.** To work together, we need to stop the personal attacks and focus on the real issues. Common ground requires a foundation of common courtesy.
    - *Go deeper*: As discussed in this chapter, this game theory strategy is most effective over the long term, so remember to start early and signal positivity.
2.  **Take action.** Being nice only goes so far. More importantly, you actually need to do the work to fix our biggest problems and invest in our future.
    - *Go deeper*: Refer to the beginnings of Chapters 6 and 7 for inspirational stories about how people with no prior political experience took personal action that led to important political movements.
3.  **Get wins quickly.** Early success builds momentum for bigger movements. This is also why quickly switching our focus from ideas to action is so important.
    - Go deeper: Part 2 begins with the advice to start small with activism. Target key issues and bills that are ready to get passed and push them over the finish line. This will give you excellent experience for a career in politics.
4.  **Think long term.** Governments are how we invest in our future. We should measure the ultimate success of our political work by its positive-sum effects over decades.
    - *Go deeper*: Part 2 ends by zooming out and considering how we could all change the world if we spent decades

working on Positive Politics. Chapter 11 gets specific, with ten huge issues that you could solve in a decade.

5. **Go direct.** Speak directly to your voters. You don't need any media access, political connections, or money to start. Use the internet to share your ideas and actions and to find your teammates, helpers, and fans.
   - *Go deeper*: We're just starting to see the power of the internet to influence voters and win elections. Start with Chapter 8 to explore how to build political power now.
6. **Be independent.** This isn't about political parties. This is about having the integrity and freedom to take any positive political action, even if it hurts special interests that might spend money in opposition to you.
   - *Go deeper*: Positive Politics is a winning strategy for people of any party and any country. See the beginning of Chapter 9 for a Positive Politics story from over two thousand years ago in ancient Rome.

### YOU DON'T HAVE TO BE PERFECTLY POSITIVE TO WIN

These Positive Politics principles work even if you don't use them perfectly. Just as the game theory of the prisoner's dilemma encourages you to get back to cooperating quickly, keep returning to these principles as soon as possible.

You also never need to be fake:

- Positive doesn't mean puff pieces. We still need journalists and activists to hold power to account and expose and protest corruption and crimes against humanity.
- Positive doesn't mean refraining from protesting. Nonviolent protests are a highly effective method for activists to enact positive change in civil rights movements.

- Positive doesn't mean always voting yes. We must make tough decisions to ensure that our future is stronger than our present and past.

It's especially hard to stay positive when the politician getting attacked is you or your family. I have read negative political attacks and lies about my dad that were bad enough to make my mom cry. I have personally faced racism and death threats online and in my mailbox at home. And I have publicly called out these cynics, critics, and corrupt people when they've attacked us multiple times. But then I do my best to go right back to being open and positive and ready to work on real issues.

## POSITIVE POLITICS IS A META-SOLUTION TO MANY OF OUR BIGGEST PROBLEMS

Negativity repels good people from politics. All the cynicism, outrage, and personal attacks only reward and attract bad actors. The best way to change politics for good is to avoid the negativity completely. Like George Bernard Shaw said, "Never wrestle with pigs. You both get dirty and the pig likes it."

We need a new movement to counter the partisanship, cynicism, and dysfunction in politics now. Positive Politics will be a unifying force that works beyond the two-party system and brings independents and apolitical people into the process. Recruiting more ambitious optimists into politics will lead to them solving many of our biggest problems. This is the most important work we can do to positively impact politics and the world.

# CHAPTER 2

★ ★ ★

# WHY POLITICS?

# 2.1

★

# POLITICS IS THE BIGGEST GAME

*"Many of our men in business...rather pride themselves on being good citizens if they even vote, the vote is still the least of their duties."*
—THEODORE ROOSEVELT, "THE DUTIES OF
AMERICAN CITIZENSHIP," 1883

When I, a young man in search of purpose, was about to graduate from college, everyone told me that the best way to change the world was through startups. You take one big idea and spend years building a company to chase that mission. So that's what I did for fourteen-plus years, co-founding three startups and a nonprofit.

These four organizations all continue to make major positive social and financial impacts. My startups raised over

$20 million, our services have been used by over one hundred million people, and the companies are now worth over $100 million. Our nonprofit Air to All rallied over five hundred volunteers from around the world to work together to design open-source medical devices during COVID-19, and we organized multicountry shipping routes to get hundreds of lifesaving medical devices to the front lines of eastern Ukraine in 2021. I'm still chairman of Labdoor, where we helped create the "lab-tested" movement and continue to drive worldwide independent testing and certifications. But if continuing to run these organizations were all I did with the rest of my career, I wouldn't feel satisfied with my impact.

As I saw our politics become increasingly negative over this time, I realized that many of our world's biggest problems can't be solved through startups. Many of my peers have spent decades building startups that are trying to change industries like healthcare and education. They may have started with a grand vision to disrupt everything, but they ended up as one more part of a software or payment flow in the existing broken system. I didn't want to fall into the same trap.

I volunteered for and led a community service nonprofit working in Detroit from 2007 to 2010, but from that time until 2016, all of my work went into my startups. By late 2016, that all changed when I helped my dad run for governor. Once I got into politics again, I saw many opportunities to help more ambitious optimists run for office and get into politics. It quickly became clear that politics was my long-term path to impact too.

## POLITICS IS ALSO THE OLDEST GAME

Long before there was technology, industry, business, or even agriculture, Neanderthals organized themselves into tribes and selected leaders not by strength but by social skill.[17] That's politics. And the first time a leader was challenged by their tribe was the first social movement. Modern politics is the result of many centuries of social and economic evolution.

The history of these social movements gives us a playbook full of ideas on how to create the future of our politics. One early example is the plebeian movement in ancient Rome, in which the Roman working class organized strikes to force the patrician elites to publish the Law of the Twelve Tables and establish equality under the law.[18] The public always outnumbers the elite, but elites win when the public is disorganized. That's why organizing collective action is an important prerequisite to building political power.

We can trace the intellectual lineage of modern activists like John Lewis and Cesar Chavez to their influences, such as Martin Luther King Jr., who was influenced by Mahatma Gandhi, who was influenced by Henry David Thoreau, who was influenced by Jesus and the Bible. Jesus, Thoreau, Gandhi, and King all fought the reigning establishments of their times and were all jailed for doing so. But their movements prevailed and now positively shape our world. Who will be the next generation of this great intellectual family tree?

## INTELLECTUAL FAMILY TREE FROM
## JESUS TO JOHN LEWIS

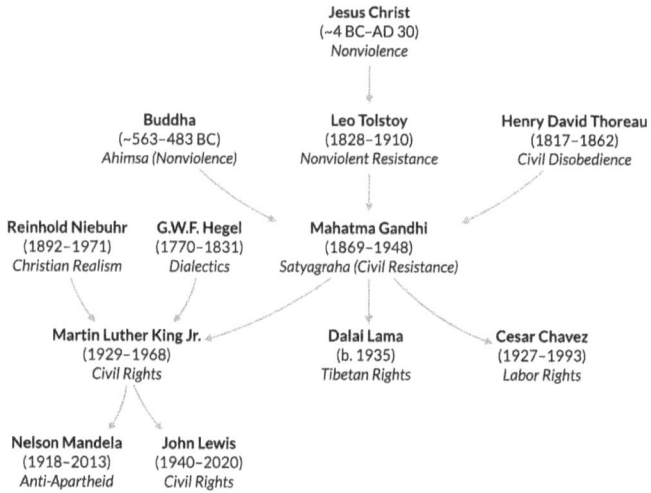

Jesus Christ
(~4 BC–AD 30)
*Nonviolence*

Buddha
(~563–483 BC)
*Ahimsa (Nonviolence)*

Leo Tolstoy
(1828–1910)
*Nonviolent Resistance*

Henry David Thoreau
(1817–1862)
*Civil Disobedience*

Reinhold Niebuhr
(1892–1971)
*Christian Realism*

G.W.F. Hegel
(1770–1831)
*Dialectics*

Mahatma Gandhi
(1869–1948)
*Satyagraha (Civil Resistance)*

Martin Luther King Jr.
(1929–1968)
*Civil Rights*

Dalai Lama
(b. 1935)
*Tibetan Rights*

Cesar Chavez
(1927–1993)
*Labor Rights*

Nelson Mandela
(1918–2013)
*Anti-Apartheid*

John Lewis
(1940–2020)
*Civil Rights*

Sources: Kathryn Selig Brown, The Metropolitan Museum of Art; Taylor Branch; Rob Sellers, Christian Ethics Today[19]

Positive Politics aims to join this lineage of great leaders and social movements by bringing nonviolent activism into the twenty-first century and fighting for abundance and freedom for all and against the forces of authoritarianism and tyranny.

## POLITICS IS HOW WE SOLVE THE
## WORLD'S BIGGEST PROBLEMS

*"The real question is what are the needs of our people? We don't need Republican roads or Democratic roads. We need roads. We don't need Republican health care or Democratic health care. We need health*

*care. We don't need Republican clean air or Democratic clean air. We all breathe the same air."*

—ARNOLD SCHWARZENEGGER, SECOND
INAUGURAL ADDRESS, 2007

Do you want every American to have access to safe roads, quality healthcare, and clean air? You can't do that through a startup. Solving fundamental issues for everyone requires systemic change. And that means getting into politics and building power, whether by organizing to advocate for a new bill or running for office yourself. I still believe startups are the fastest way to fix any one specific problem. But we shouldn't confuse point solutions with systemic solutions. So if you want to solve big problems for everyone, you need to get into politics.

It's easy to be cynical about politics. Any enterprise built to solve all problems for all people will be inefficient. Our governments feed, educate, and protect millions of people every day. If we focus only on the waste, we are like dinner guests complaining about the scraps in the trash instead of complimenting the cook on the meal. That's why a key strategy of Positive Politics is to consistently focus on the fundamental issues that our governments can and do solve every day. We should give politics more credit for its successes, both big and small.

## LET'S DISPEL THE BIGGEST MYTHS ABOUT POLITICS

### 1. DON'T GOVERNMENTS WASTE OUR MONEY?

Governments are, in many ways, an insurance policy. We pay firefighters even on days when there are no fires because it's critical for them to be ready when fires do occur. The same is true for national defense and pandemic preparedness and many other government expenditures. You don't cancel your insurance just because you were healthy last year. We should treat government spending like insurance for and investment in our future because that's what it is.

Governments are also the first investors for much of our best science and technology, from famous examples like the internet, GPS, and the Human Genome Project to lesser-known breakthroughs like early solar cell and renewable energy research funded by the Department of Energy and foundational biotech research funded by the National Institutes of Health. Even high-risk early-stage venture capitalists invest over ten-year fund cycles. These fundamental breakthroughs, however, each took over thirty years to reach mainstream adoption. Only governments are capable of investing decades into the future for this fundamental research.

## 2. AREN'T ALL POLITICIANS CORRUPT?

There are both bad reasons (e.g., power) and good reasons (e.g., altruism) to run for politics. People who blindly believe that all politicians are corrupt are resigning themselves to be ruled by power-hungry politicians. Noted cynic Plato claimed that "the greatest of penalties is being ruled by a worse man if one is not willing to rule oneself."[20] But you don't have to be this cynical to get into politics!

The truth is that even the worst politicians don't get into this game for the money. They do it for fame. The people who are getting rich from politics now are the corporate donors. Campaign contributions are just the tool they use to promote and control their favorite politicians. The solution is simple—campaign finance reform. More on that in section 11.2.

### 3. ISN'T POLITICS FULL OF CONSPIRACIES?

Fear of the system itself often keeps individuals out of politics. Some people truly believe that all politicians are evil members of some global conspiracy to control the world. The truth is much less sinister, and frankly boring. I've met people at all levels of government both in private and public, been inside the White House and the US Capitol many times, and been in those smoke-filled rooms (many congressional leadership offices really do reek of cigars, especially during key votes). But the reality is that most of the politicians you see on TV are normal people who are driven by power and ego. We need more ambitious optimists like you to get into politics and make the government and our country better!

### 4. ISN'T POLITICS TOO SLOW?

I also used to believe that politics moved too slowly. It took me over ten years working in startups to realize that changing any large industry takes decades. Now when idealistic founders come to me with a big startup idea to change an important regulated industry like education or healthcare, I first ask them whether they're willing to commit over ten years to this mission. When they say yes, I ask them if they'd also be willing to commit three to five years to try to pass key legislation that could permanently fix the problem they want to solve. The former gets the media attention, but the latter often makes a more immediate and profound impact.

### 5. WHAT IF I GET ATTACKED?

You don't have to give up your privacy to get into politics. Our stereotypical image of politics is the US presidency, a 24/7/365 job where you get no personal life and you and your family are constantly vilified and in danger. So it's easy to be turned off by the whole idea of entering politics. But there are literally millions of other Americans like you working in our politics and government every day and living private lives with major public impact. We should celebrate these people and give them more media attention. And even if you do get attacked, the many Positive Politics strategies introduced in Chapter 1 and discussed throughout this book will help you deflect this negativity and get back to your important work.

## YOU ARE ALREADY IN POLITICS
## WHETHER YOU LIKE IT OR NOT

As Pericles said, "Just because you do not take an interest in politics doesn't mean politics won't take an interest in you." Don't be afraid of criticism—pseudonymity and confidence can defuse it. Don't be afraid of failure—optimism and perseverance can overcome it. And don't be afraid of the work—organizing and activism can handle it. Part 2 of this book will explain how to do each of these things. All you need to get started in politics is a desire to help and a willingness to work.

Don't let politics scare you. That's what the establishment wants. Politics is a simple numbers game. First you win elections by getting at least one vote more than the other candidates, and then you pass bills by getting at least one vote more than the other side. Along the way, you'll become proficient at using your ideas to organize, your voice to inspire, and your actions to improve lives. We all must take a more active role in our politics now—our future depends on it. Let's go fight!

## 2.2

★

# GOVERNMENT IS GOOD

*"Let us not despair but act. Let us not seek the Republican answer or the Democratic answer but the right answer. Let us not seek to fix the blame for the past—let us accept our own responsibility for the future."*

—JOHN F. KENNEDY, 1958

At 7:15 p.m. ET on September 11, 2001, members of the House and the Senate stood on the US Capitol steps in solidarity with our nation, which was under attack. Planes hijacked by terrorists had hit the World Trade Center and the Pentagon that morning, and there was no promise that Congress was safe at that moment. But still, they stood openly in front of the world, not as Republicans and Democrats but as Americans. After a moment of silence, our representatives started singing "God Bless America," like parents who had been fighting all day but then came together to put their beloved children to bed.[21] This is the positive power of politics.

A moment of silence before members of Congress sing "God Bless America" on September 11, 2011.
Source: C-SPAN, 2001[22]


## GOVERNMENTS ARE THE BEST WAY TO SOLVE BIG COLLECTIVE ACTION PROBLEMS

Collective action problems arise when individuals who would benefit from working together don't because it's hard to coordinate the costs and work. Public goods like defense, education, and healthcare are classic positive-sum solutions to these problems. Everyone benefits when children have better access to schools and hospitals. And these are not just liberal issues. Emergency services and national defense, including police, firefighters, and the military, are all public goods too. Governments are how we organize our resources to solve these problems.

In moments of crisis, politicians from different parties and countries have worked together to solve collective action problems. Pollution is a classic example. Before the 1960s, any person or company could pollute our air or water and hurt their whole community without costing themselves. Then the Clean Air Act of 1970 and Clean Water Act of 1972 funded testing (to find the sources of pollution), standards (to set safety limits), and regulations (to enforce those standards). Since 1970, emissions of the six major air pollutants have dropped by over 70 percent, even as our population has grown by over 60 percent and our economy has grown by over 300 percent.[23]

**Change in Gross Domestic Product, US Population, Energy Consumption, and Aggregate Emissions: 1980–2023**

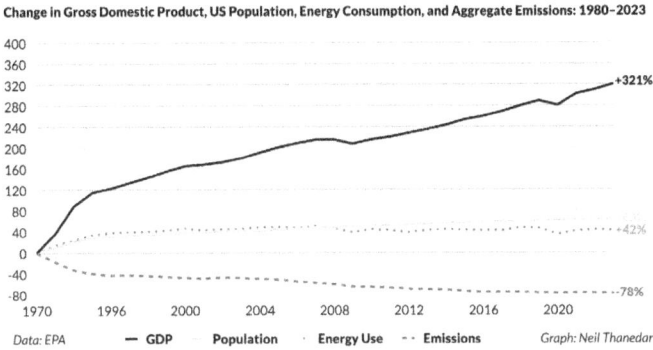

Source: Environmental Protection Agency, 2024[24]

Both the Clean Air Act and the Clean Water Act relied on bipartisan support and coordination between the Democrat-led Congress, especially Senator Edmund Muskie (D-ME), and the Republican-led White House, with President Richard Nixon establishing the Environmental Protection Agency (EPA) in 1970 after signing the Clean Air Act. We all still benefit from these acts today.

Bipartisan coordination happens more often than you might think. Partisan battles like debt ceiling negotiations get most of the political media attention, but GovTrack found that 59 percent of substantive bills in Congress in 2024 passed with "very bipartisan" support (over three hundred votes out of 435 in the House).[25] While the daily news loves to focus on angry partisanship, the history books remember the bipartisan legislation that truly shapes our future. You can be part of that history and future by engaging in Positive Politics and working to pass new laws!

Solving new existential dangers in AI, biotech, and climate change will also require political solutions to collective action problems. For example, investing in research now to prevent the next pandemic could save millions of lives and trillions of dollars. Governments are uniquely positioned to invest in long-term projects that benefit everyone. This is the very definition of a public good. These investments ought to be nonpartisan. Positive Politicians should focus on how to most efficiently provide more public goods to build trust in government.

## GOVERNMENTS PROVIDE ESSENTIAL SERVICES TO MILLIONS OF AMERICANS EVERY DAY

*"This is what I give. I give an expression of care every day to each child."*

—FRED ROGERS, SENATE TESTIMONY ON PBS FUNDING, 1969

Every weekday morning, my kids take a public bus down a public road to a public school. Along the way, they'll pass their favorite public park, cross a public bridge over a public highway, and get to school in about fifteen minutes, where they'll get two free meals and a full day of math, reading, art, science, and exercise. We don't pay for any of these services when we use them. My taxes help cover the costs of all these public goods and more. It's important to celebrate all the positive value we get from our politics.

Behind everything we call "free" or "public" is a team of government workers doing the work so we can all benefit. Over fifty million American children attend our public schools.[26] Welfare programs like Social Security and Medicaid provide a safety net for millions of elderly and disabled Americans. We all benefit constantly from clean air and water. And over two million active duty and reserve military personnel defend our freedom.

So many of the people we call "heroes" are government workers. Our government is truly "of the people, by the people, for the people" in the words of Abraham Lincoln. When we celebrate our teachers, firefighters, police officers, military members, and social workers, let's remember that this is our government at work.

## GOVERNMENTS HAVE MORE LEVERAGE THAN ANY OTHER SECTOR TO IMPROVE OUR LIVES

While companies can succeed by serving less than 1 percent of the population, governments are responsible for serving 100 percent of us. Over 80 percent of all American children go to public schools.[27] Twenty-four percent of all Americans receive Medicaid or Children's Health Insurance Program (CHIP) health coverage, another 20 percent are covered by Medicare, and 20 percent of all Americans are currently on Social Security.[28] We all benefit from a safer, happier, and more prosperous world when our people are healthy and educated. If you want to provide healthcare to all Americans, a startup cannot solve that problem. It must be done by our government.

The US government is also responsible for many of our largest scientific and technological breakthroughs of the last century. The Defense Advanced Research Projects Agency (DARPA) created ARPANET, the basis for the internet; helped develop GPS and weather satellites; and even awarded Moderna $25 million in 2013 to develop mRNA vaccines seven years before we needed them.[29] The NIH funded the creation of the Human Genome Project and led advances in the treatment of cancer, HIV, and AIDs. 99.4 percent of all drugs approved by the FDA between 2010 and 2019 were derived from NIH-funded research.[30] And NASA technology, like medical imaging, water filtration, and solar cells, make life on Earth better too. Government investments in science and technology have led to massive positive returns for America and the world.

## GOVERNMENTS AND STARTUPS NEED EACH OTHER TO BE SUCCESSFUL

Government investments also accelerate startup success. For example, the High-Performance Computing Act of 1991 (HPCA) helped fund the National Center for Supercomputing Applications (NCSA), where the first public web browser, Mosaic, was created. Mosaic and Netscape co-founder Marc Andreessen said, "If it had been left to private industry, it wouldn't have happened...at least, not until years later."[31] And HPCA creator Al Gore said, "Government has supplied the initial flicker—and individuals and companies have provided the creativity and innovation that kindled that spark into a blaze of progress and productivity."[32] This partnership between public and private innovators is key to America's success.

We need our government to keep catalyzing scientific and technological advances. DARPA should be investing in the latest AI, semiconductor, and computing technologies. NIH should once again invest in solutions for future pandemics. And NASA should be researching alternative power generation and storage solutions. We need to invest more government funding with a startup-like mindset, which considers a 90 percent failure rate among projects to be acceptable as long as the biggest successes generate more value than our overall initial investments. This is how we get the massive positive returns of projects like vaccines and the internet.

We need to dedicate more public resources to funding this innovation. A great national example of this is NIH's Seed Fund, which provides over $1.4 billion in nondilutive funds every year to support small business research and development. However, China's government venture capital funds have invested $912 billion in the last decade into AI alone.[33] With the US federal government spending trillions of dollars each year overall, we need to redirect more of this funding to the technologies, startups, and individuals inventing the future.

## OUR GOVERNMENT WOULD BE EVEN BETTER WITH YOU IN IT!

Governments are just groups of people doing work for us. Right now, those groups may not include you, so it's easy to be frustrated by the lack of progress in politics. Use this energy for good. This book is here to help you get in the game and start improving your community, one issue at a time. The work we call politics is all around us—you can join anytime.

Go meet your local politicians, like your mayor and city council representative. You'll find that most of them are good, genuine people who earnestly got into politics to make a positive difference in their communities. You'll also hear them complain about the complexities of the system and how tiring it is to raise money and campaign constantly. Don't hate the players; change the game. Let's all fight for Positive Politics!

# CHAPTER 3

*  *  *

# WHY NOW?

## 3.1

☆

# YOU'RE YOUNGER
# THAN YOU THINK

*"If not us, then who? If not now, then when?"*

—JOHN LEWIS

If you ever feel like you're old, visit Congress. Less than 7 percent of voting members are under forty years old. And the average age has actually dropped over the last two Congresses, from 58.9 to 57.5.[34] These age demographics spotlight the fact that politics makes for a great second act in anyone's life. If you have spent ten-plus years in an industry like Silicon Valley, Big Law, Wall Street, Hollywood, or pro sports, where your "prime" working years are usually defined as your twenties and thirties, transitioning into politics could be perfect for you now.

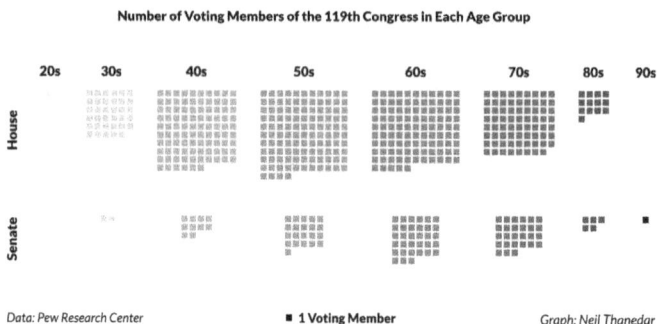

Number of Voting Members of the 119th Congress in Each Age Group

Data: Pew Research Center ■ 1 Voting Member Graph: Neil Thanedar

Source: Drew DeSilver, Pew Research Center, 2025[35]

## POLITICS CAN BE YOUR "SECOND PRIME" AT ANY AGE

A lot of us rush through our twenties and thirties trying to accomplish as much as we can, as quickly as possible—chasing more money, more fame, more responsibility. This was certainly true in my case. Being a twenty-one-year-old founder and CEO was cool. But by the time I hit my mid-thirties, with a bald head and bags under my eyes, I knew that my titles just meant I had the longest hours and the most stress. Around this time, fear also started creeping in. I wondered, "Is this it? Am I going to be doing the same thing for my whole life?"

A midlife crisis is a period of questioning your identity and searching for meaning. Often a major life event—marriage, kids, divorce, the death of a parent—triggers this crisis. For me, this was turning thirty-six (the age my mom was when she died), having my third kid, launching my third startup, and feeling like I still hadn't lived up to my full potential.

This kind of crisis reminds us of our mortality and makes us feel like time is running out. But it also pushes us to find a new path with higher impact. My transformation happened gradually, as I had volunteered in politics for many years. But as I saw the positive impact that even a few hours of my work each week could do in politics, I kept getting pulled in deeper. Once I started getting stuff done and building power in politics, I knew it was my highest calling. This is what inspired me to make politics my second career.

We all have more time than we think, especially for work like activism and politics. When my dad entered politics at sixty-one, an age when many other people retire, it was easy to question whether he could make that transition and start a new and very public career. But this past decade has proved him right. He's had more energy, worked harder, and traveled more during these years than ever before, all because he now has a higher purpose. And the timing is now perfect for him, with his kids all grown up, his business successfully sold, and his nest egg secured. Now he has all the time and resources needed to take his biggest shots in politics.

## DON'T BE AFRAID OF POLITICS

Successful people in their first careers often hesitate to transition into politics because they're afraid of starting at the beginning and they're scared of failing. You might be picturing yourself getting coffee for a congressman or losing the first race you find and then never running again. Maybe it seems easier to stay in your first career for life, compounding the gains of your initial success. What would happen if you did the same thing for the next ten years? I bet you would be richer. But would you have ten new years of experience, or would this time be spent a lot like your last ten years? What's worse: trying something new and failing or never trying at all?

It's normal to take many shots on the way to success. Startup culture has done a great job of normalizing the idea that up to

90 percent of new businesses fail. Founders are encouraged to create many startups over their careers, and we celebrate all entrepreneurs, not just the winners. We need this same mindset in politics, where in every election, at least 50 percent of the candidates will lose. It helps to have a startup or sporting mindset to winning and losing in politics.

Getting into politics will challenge you. It will require you to learn new things and meet new people. You might have to call and email and meet your local politicians to get them to vote on an important bill. You might have to get out of your comfort zone and knock on strangers' doors for a good cause. You might have to learn how to stand on stage and confidently give a speech to rally hundreds or thousands of people. On the other side of your fear is the confidence that you will be living a new life with more meaning and impact.

## WINNING IN POLITICS IS SIMPLE—GET STARTED AND DON'T QUIT

It doesn't matter if you feel like you're too early or too late for politics—just get started. As the proverb says, "The best time to plant a tree was twenty years ago; the second-best time is now." And don't be afraid of losing. Politics can be tough, but it's only over when you quit!

First, you wouldn't really start at the beginning in politics. If you have leadership experience and business, legal, or public service skills, those can be applied directly to political campaigns and nonprofits. Operationally, startups and campaigns have similar functions, including fundraising, marketing, and sales. Lean into your strengths when you first get into politics.

One easy way to get into politics is to find the same job you already have but for a campaign. Already leading marketing at a startup? You'd be a great communications director. Startup founders make great political candidates, and both CEOs and COOs make great campaign managers. And this strategy does not only apply to business experience. Educators make great politicians because so much of activism and politics relies on informing the public in an interesting way. The biggest commonality here is an ambitious optimist's desire to positively impact the world.

Second, if you lose, you can run again! My dad lost his first race but won his next three, including the last two for US Congress. Current members of Congress Ro Khanna (D-CA), David Valadao (R-CA), Hillary Scholten (D-MI), and Tom Barrett (R-MI) all lost general elections for their exact seat before running again in the following election and winning. Every US president since Dwight D. Eisenhower, the general and World War II hero with no prior political experience, lost at least one election before winning the presidency. Their careers would've been over at that loss if they had quit. But they kept going, and the rest is history.

Now is a perfect time for you to get into politics too. Are you searching for more meaning in your life but feel like the world's on fire? Stop waiting for the world to change—do the work to fix it. We will be the ones to lead society from the current crisis to our next awakening.

☆

# THE THREE BIG POSITIVE TRENDS

*"Generals always prepare to fight the last war, especially if they won it."*

—GEORGE CLEMENCEAU

About every eighty years, America goes through a major crisis. It's been 242 years since the Revolutionary War, 159 years since the Civil War, and 80 years since the end of World War II. History is repeating again. We're back in crisis mode now.

To think positively, each of these crises ended with an optimistic period with new leaders, more babies, advances in political liberty, and new waves of technology. While we are deep into a negative cycle now, multiple key political pendulums are swinging in a positive direction. Positive Politicians should be ready to ride these trends to wins and impact in the coming decades.

## HOW LONG WILL THE CURRENT NEGATIVITY LAST?

The last three presidential elections—in 2016, 2020, and 2024—have been framed almost entirely negatively. Each candidate tried to portray the other as the ultimate threat to America and portrayed themselves as the only antidote. As we discussed in Chapter 1, this recent political negativity and cynicism goes back as far as 1995 to the Clinton versus Gingrich rivalry. Even the positivity of the 2008 presidential election was quickly lost in the 2009 fight over healthcare reform. We're now more than thirty years into a negative political cycle.

But the history and future of politics are positive. Talk to the vast majority of Americans—independents, Republicans, and Democrats. They don't care who's right about these attacks. They just want better jobs, housing, healthcare, and education. The public wants Positive Politicians—people who are motivated to solve problems and driven to fight for a better future. The next decade will see the political pendulum to swing back this positivity.

Millennials grew up in a time full of crises, from 2001 to today, experiencing everything from 9/11 to the global financial crisis to COVID-19, so it's easy for them to believe that this era of fear, negative partisanship, and politics will never end. But there's also a long history of positive presidents, from Obama and Clinton to Reagan and Eisenhower to both Roosevelts, just in the last hundred years. We're just one thermostatic swing away from another long Positive Politics era!

## THREE MAJOR TRENDS ALL MAKE NOW THE
## PERFECT TIME FOR POSITIVE POLITICAL CHANGE

1. Thermostatic regulation will swing us from anti-establishment negativity to prosocial positivity.
2. Rising inequality over the last fifty years will make way for rising abundance in the next fifty years.
3. A "Fourth Turning" will take us from the current crisis to the next high.

## 1. THERMOSTATIC REGULATION: POLITICS
## WILL SWING BACK TO POSITIVITY

The public acts as a thermostat, tempering the extremes of politicians in either direction. This thermostatic model was introduced in Christopher Wlezien's 1995 study on changes in public preferences for government spending.[36] A decades-long index of public policy polling by James Stimson tracking shifts in support for key issues over the last thirteen presidencies confirms this thermostatic trend.[37]

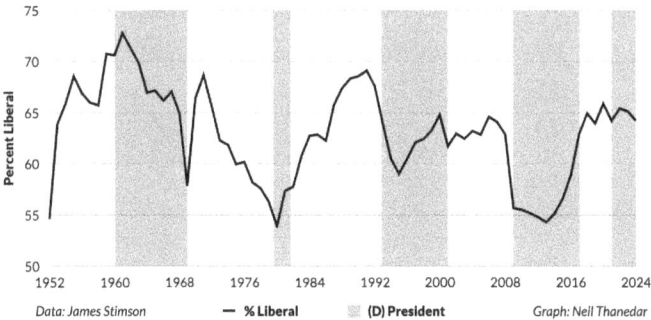

Data: James Stimson  — % Liberal  (D) President  Graph: Neil Thanedar

Source: James Stimson, 2023[38]

We can predict multiple upcoming political swings based on these trends. First, when a presidential term has been focused on cutting government expenses, we should expect the next incoming president to focus on how to responsibly add government services. Second, after an extended period of political negativity, Positive Politicians will stand out from the crowd and will increasingly be seen as the proper antidote for our current political problems.

Of course, the pendulum can always swing away from us later, especially if our government is ineffective while we're in charge. But as long as we focus on the fundamentals of Positive Politics, we will earn the public trust we need to endure these cycles and keep winning.

## 2. RISING ABUNDANCE: MULTIPLE ECONOMIC WAVES WILL LIFT ALL BOATS

Economic growth also rises and falls in waves. Soviet economist Nikolai Kondratiev famously theorized in his 1936 book *The Long Waves in Economic Life* that the world economy goes through forty- to sixty-year cycles of prosperity, recession, depression, and innovation that follow technological waves. These economic cycles closely match and drive political cycles.

Approximate Timing and Amplitude of Kondratiev Waves: 1780–2050

PROGRESS

Biological Power?

Computing Power

Combustion Power

Electric Power

Steam Power

Water Power

P  R  D  I

1780  1800  1820  1840  1860  1880  1900  1920  1940  1960  1980  2000  2020  2040

P = Prosperity     R = Recession     D = Depression     I = Innovation

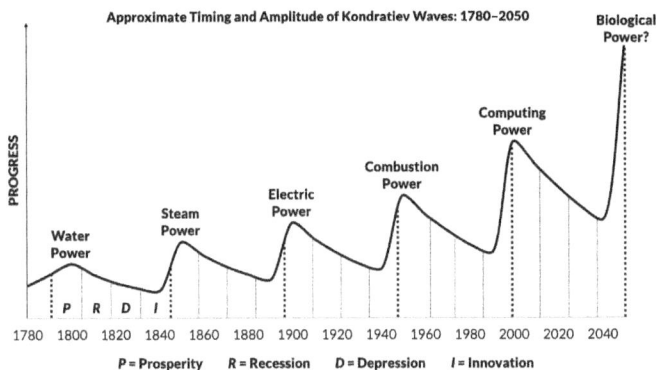

Source: Martin Hilbert, 2020[39]

The world is now thirty to forty years into its information technology cycle, which is why we're feeling the negative side of this wave now as we start to see the diminishing returns of the internet era. But the next wave of technology, promising abundance of energy, medicine, and food through new AI and biotech breakthroughs, is already rising. This next wave of prosperity will further energize our Positive Politics movement in the coming decades, and Positive Politicians need to focus on democratizing access to this new abundance through public goods.

Technological advances can cause the costs of major commodities to drop by more than 99 percent in a decade. In information technology, this is called Moore's law, Gordon Moore's idea that the number of transistors on a microchip doubles every eighteen months. This massive cost trend has powered most of our current technological cycle by making fitting computing power into progressively smaller devices ever cheaper. Now over 60 percent of the global population owns a smartphone, which has revolutionized worldwide information and economic access.

This same commodification will happen this century with fundamentals like energy, water, and medicine. What happens when solar power becomes too cheap to meter and battery capacity improves so much that we start freely powering everything with the sun? What happens when water desalination costs 1 percent of the current price and everyone in the world can freely access clean water? What happens when personalized medicines cost hundreds of dollars per person per year, not millions? So much of our world's conflicts are based on a scarcity of resources. The technological advances of the next fifty years could eliminate the causes of many wars and economic conflicts and help Positive Politicians successfully lead us through peacetime.

### 3. FOURTH TURNING: WINTER IS HERE— BUT THE NEXT SPRING IS NEAR

*"Hard times create strong men, strong men create good times, good times create weak men, and weak men create hard times."*

—G. MICHAEL HOPF, *THOSE WHO REMAIN*

In their landmark 1997 book *The Fourth Turning*, William Strauss and Neil Howe theorized that history moves in roughly eighty-year cycles, from High to Awakening to Unraveling to Crisis and back again. America's first three crises led to the Revolutionary War in the 1770s, the Civil War in the 1860s, and World War II in the 1940s. What will be the culmination of our current crisis? And who will lead us into our next positive cycle?

We are in another Fourth Turning now. The common thread of the societal response to the 9/11 terrorist attacks, global financial crisis, and COVID-19 pandemic is an unraveling of the public's trust in our major institutions. This has led to a crisis of authority where presidents and politicians from both parties openly use their power and insider information for personal gain. Cynicism and corruption are rampant again.

In 1997, Strauss and Howe predicted that a new generation raised at the turn of this century in a period of societal upheaval and cultural crises would grow up to become a new hero generation, like the GI Generation eighty years earlier. They named this generation "millennials," and the label stuck. But Strauss and Howe's prediction of the rise of the millennials is still underreported and just proving itself true now. It's long past time for millennials to live up to their potential and lead society from crisis to awakening again.

In his 2023 book, *The Fourth Turning Is Here*, Neil Howe confirms that we are in this Crisis phase now, with millennials poised to be the "Next Great Generation." But we can't do this alone. Just like the GI Generation before us, we'll need a multigenerational coalition to fight this crisis. Older generations need to use more of their power too. Younger generations need to stop waiting for the world to change. Together, we will usher in the Positive Politics era!

Read *The Fourth Turning* by William Strauss and Neil Howe to learn more about these eighty-year cycles and *The Fourth Turning Is Here* for Neil Howe's prediction of how the current crisis will culminate by the early 2030s.

## NOW IS THE PERFECT TIME TO START THIS MOVEMENT

This is a particularly good time to start the Positive Politics movement. Three straight presidential elections have been defined by Republican Donald Trump's negativity toward many groups and the Democratic party's negativity toward Trump. But 2028 will be the start of a new era in politics, with Trump being term-limited. Republicans, Democrats, and independents have an opportunity to positively influence that election now.

Both parties should plan for their post-Trump future. For Republicans, this means stopping the negative politics that helped them win in 2024 and starting to deliver results for all. For Democrats, this means focusing on policies over politics, making our government more efficient, and delivering more services, especially in state and local governments where they still have control. And for independents, this means taking direct political action beyond voting—working with people of both parties to get things done. Americans across the political spectrum want more positivity now and this is our chance to make it happen.

To exit this negative era in politics, we need a clear positive vision for the future. We can't just swing politics toward another kind of negativity. We need to build momentum through a series of positive-sum actions to prove we can lead America out of this period. We know that much of the negativity in politics is fake. So being nice and thinking of the long term is still a winning strategy in both game theory and American politics. We can usher in another era of Positive Politics if we deliver real positive solutions for America.

It may feel like we've been stuck in negative politics forever. But if you examine history, politics has had many seasons of positivity. We are due for another historical Positive Politics movement.

As the poet June Jordan said, "We are the ones we've been waiting for." It's our time to lead. Will you answer the call?

# CHAPTER 4

☆ ☆ ☆

# WHY YOU?

## 4.1

☆

# OUR HEROES HAD HUMBLE ORIGINS

*"I was born and have ever remained in the most humble walks of life."*
—ABRAHAM LINCOLN, FIRST POLITICAL ANNOUNCEMENT, 1832

Michael was born in Atlanta, Georgia, a middle child who was somewhat rebellious but still maintained a B+ average in high school. As a freshman in college, he initially wanted to be a lawyer, but quickly changed majors and showed little interest in getting a real job, pursuing a master's and a PhD because he didn't know what to do with his life. At twenty-four, his dream was to be a professor. His father convinced him to work in the family business for a summer, where he excelled but bristled at being in his dad's shadow. He got married, had his first child, and finally got his first job at the age of twenty-five. He seemed destined for a quiet, private life. But that all changed one year later, in 1955, when the man everyone had once called Young Mike emerged as the leader of the Montgomery bus boycott. Now known as Reverend Dr. Martin Luther King Jr., he was just twenty-six at the time.

We tend to imagine our heroes as ancient mythical figures, as seen in pictures and paintings at the end of their careers. But if you go back and read their real stories, you'll find that most of them led normal private lives before suddenly entering public life by accepting an immediate challenge in front of them. When you look to great politicians and activists for inspiration, don't compare yourself to their statues and quotes. See how much you relate to their early private lives, before the fame, when they, too, were searching for meaning. It can be more motivating to realize that they weren't born superheroes; they were real people who took action on a local issue and then kept working until they changed the world.

John Lewis originally wanted to be a preacher and a teacher. The 1955 Montgomery bus boycott inspired a fifteen-year-old Lewis to start preaching publicly. And after being denied admission to the teaching school Troy University at age eighteen, Lewis wrote to King about suing the university for discrimination and King agreed to meet the young Lewis.[40] King warned Lewis that a lawsuit could put his family in danger and instead encouraged him to go to a historically black college and become an activist. Lewis helped organize the Nashville sit-in movement as a student, which led to the desegregation of lunch counters in the city after Lewis and his fellow activists had been arrested for their nonviolent protests numerous times.[41] After over thirty years as an activist, John Lewis became a US congressman in 1987 and served until his death in 2020.

Imagine a world where Martin Luther King Jr. and John

Lewis got "real" jobs. Even if they had founded billion-dollar startups, written bestselling books, and starred in the biggest TV shows and movies, it's hard to envision any other path that would have led to them having a greater impact on the world than their real lives in politics and activism did. How different would the rest of your life be if you chose to get into politics too?

You may think you're nothing like these leaders. But even MLK took a long, winding path to activism. At twenty-four, King was getting a PhD, largely to avoid becoming a pastor at his dad's church. He didn't find his true calling until joining his local Montgomery bus boycott at the age of twenty-six. He was a young man in search of purpose. That 381-day protest changed his life.

Read *Parting the Waters* by Taylor Branch for more on young MLK's life.

I've met many ambitious people in search of their purpose. They want to find more meaning in their work but know their company isn't saving the world. So they promise that they'll work hard at this job for five to ten more years and then they'll follow their true calling. But somehow life—marriage, kids, lifestyle creep—always gets in the way of that big leap. I know many people who are much richer than I am and who are still stuck in that rat race at over fifty years old, constantly chasing bigger homes and better private schools.

Too many people live deferred life plans; they promise themselves they'll focus on money now and impact later. But life is often shorter than you think, and the sacrifices you make now don't always pay off. As David Clarke said, "twenty years from now, the only people who will remember that you worked late are your kids." It's not worth wasting a single minute working on something that you wouldn't be proud of showing your kids.

There is a different, better path available to anyone at any time. You can get into politics now, dedicating even an hour a week to taking action. This could be volunteering for your favorite candidate, joining a community organization, participating in a local protest, or attending and speaking at a public hearing. I also started small in politics, volunteering on the side, learning in my spare time. But a decade of working on both startups and politics taught me that the latter is where I find the most meaning and energy, so now I'm all in on politics. I believe that your life would be so much fuller and more exciting if you got deeper into politics too.

## IT'S NEVER TOO EARLY OR TOO LATE TO GET INTO POLITICS

You can get started in politics at any age. Politics makes for a great first career or a great second or third career. You can keep your job and volunteer in politics at the same time. You can be a public candidate or a private advisor. You can work locally or travel nationally. There are many effective paths into politics that can work around your life.

If you're Gen Z and aren't even old enough to vote, you can be an activist. If you're a millennial who's worried about money, you can get a job in politics. If you're Gen X and stuck in a career that's high in money and low in meaning, running for office can reinvigorate your passion for impact. And if you're a boomer thinking it's too late for you to get started, just look at the many examples of politicians getting started in their sixties or later!

I've seen one of these stories up close. As a sixty-one-year-old immigrant entrepreneur with an accent, my dad never thought he could win an election in America. When we started working on his first race, he gave us less than a 1 percent chance of winning. But what we learned over the next two years led to us going into our second election day leading every poll and winning by 15 percent. In his eight-plus years in politics, he's earned more 500,000 total votes in Michigan in four primary elections and three general elections, winning six of those seven races and becoming a US congressman. You can get a long way in politics if you just get started and don't quit!

In all five of the following examples, which I will explore in Part 2 of this book, individuals started small, found initial traction and excitement, and then committed fully and publicly to their new mission. None were rich or famous before they started. The most striking similarity is that all five leaders used their words to organize powerful action—changing laws, constitutions, governments, and our country itself. And they all started locally, committing to make change at home before trying to change the world.

### EXAMPLES OF POSITIVE POLITICS AT ANY AGE

- Gregory Watson, at age nineteen, got a C grade on a college term paper that explained his idea for a new constitutional amendment requiring congressional pay raises to only go into effect after the next election, ensuring accountability. After a ten-year campaign led by Watson, the 27th Amendment was officially ratified in 1982. Learn more about Watson's journey to change the US Constitution and his grade in section 7.1.
- Katie Fahey created a movement at age twenty-seven to end gerrymandering in Michigan and helped collect more than 400,000

signatures and 2,500,000 votes to pass a new constitutional amendment establishing independent redistricting. The organization she
created, Voters Not Politicians, has now led three major statewide
ballot proposals. Fahey's story, in Chapter 6, is a great example of
how to get into politics through activism.

- Dolores Huerta started a labor strike against grape growers in California at age thirty-five. Five years later, this had led to new contracts,
safety rules, and a health fund for workers. And five years after that,
Huerta helped pass the first collective bargaining law in California.
Now over ninety-five years old, she still advocates for social justice
through the Dolores Huerta Foundation. We'll return to Huerta's
story at the beginning of the book's conclusion.

- Ellen Malcolm launched EMILYs List at age thirty-eight, with a goal to
elect more women in politics. Malcolm's strategy of bundling small
donations from hundreds of thousands of members led to the election of more than a thousand women in state and local races, along
with 175 US congresswomen. EMILYs List is still a key accelerator
for women in politics over forty years later. Malcolm's story kicks off
section 8.2 to inspire you to organize collective action.

- Doris "Granny D" Haddock became an activist at age fifty, organizing
tea parties to protest nuclear weapons testing. She went on to be an
activist for over fifty more years, and her advocacy helped lead to
the signing of the Partial Test Ban Treaty in 1963 and the Bipartisan
Campaign Reform Act in 2002. Haddock's story in section 7.2 reminds
us that it's never too late to get into activism or stay active in politics.

## GREAT POLITICIANS CAN COME FROM ANYWHERE

I've met many wonderful people in public service and the private sector who I believe would be amazing politicians. When I
encourage them to get into politics, their first reaction is often

to point out that they don't see anyone else like them running. That's a good thing! We need new politicians and the different perspectives that these varied lives would bring to our government—this could be you.

I've helped my dad make this transformation over the last decade. Despite all his career successes, he's making the biggest positive impact of his life now, in politics, at a time when most of his peers are retired. That's true success.

Seeing the positive impact of my work as a volunteer inspired me to go into politics full time too, becoming executive director of the Michigan Campaign Finance Network to fight dark money in politics. And now I'm publishing this book to kickstart the Positive Politics movement. Politics is now both my passion and my career, and I'm loving it.

**YOU CAN BECOME ONE OF THESE LEADERS IF YOU GET INTO POLITICS NOW**

Imagine how different your life will be in ten years if you get into politics now. Even if you're already rich and successful, I bet that your life will be more positively defined by what you do in politics than by any other work.

Politics doesn't just add lines to your résumé; it adds lines to your eulogy. What could you accomplish in the rest of your life in politics? Let's find out.

## 4.2

## USE YOUR SKILLS FOR GREATNESS

*"Your work is going to fill a large part of your life, and the only way to be truly satisfied is to do what you believe is great work. And the only way to do great work is to love what you do."*
—STEVE JOBS, STANFORD COMMENCEMENT ADDRESS, 2005

### WHY ARE SO MANY RICH, SUCCESSFUL PEOPLE DEPRESSED?

In every case I've seen, successful people struggle when they're not striving for a bigger mission. They think that having a bigger house, nicer cars, and fancier vacations will make them happy, but what they really want is to succeed at something important—to be the main character in a movie worth watching.

After spending our twenties and thirties chasing careers and wealth, actually getting to the finish line of financial security can feel empty. What's next? Creating another startup to add another zero to your bank account? When will that end?

The pursuit of money creates golden handcuffs that keep ambitious people from doing what they really want to do. We need to free ourselves from these constraints to reach our highest potential. Most of what we dream of doing doesn't cost much money. We don't need more money; we want the freedom that money can buy.

What would you do if you won the lottery? You wouldn't just sit on the beach and do nothing for the rest of your life. You'd be free to try your biggest, boldest ideas. What if you were to live like that today? Take that leap and make your dreams real now.

I remember waking up one morning to start my new job as executive director for a nonpartisan nonprofit fighting dark money in politics. I went from making $180,000 per year plus founder equity at my last startup to $60,000 per year with no benefits at this nonprofit. But I remember being energized by one simple idea: politics was now my full-time job.

I had spent nearly a decade volunteering for political campaigns, and a decade before that, I had started volunteering for community organizations. I'd been working in politics and activism for free. Now it's my career. There's an energy that comes from aligning your internal mission with your external work. No amount of money can buy this energy. But when you align your internal and external, magic happens.

How much greater an impact could you make if you got more politically active now? Don't just envision a year or two from now. Imagine dedicating a significant slice of the rest of your life to public service. What issues would you choose to focus on? How many people could you help? Start local. Where in your city is this work being done? When is the next event? Your political journey starts here.

Ambitious optimism is the antidote to the sadness of success. There are always bigger problems to solve in politics. How many potential political leaders have we lost to the pursuit of money and fame? Don't follow them into the rat race. Get started in politics now and see how this work energizes you to solve the world's biggest problems.

## RECRUITING MORE AMBITIOUS OPTIMISTS WILL MAKE OUR POLITICS BETTER

We need new people like you in our politics. Everyone has specific life experiences that inform their beliefs. You know how to best help your family and community. Tapping into new talent and ideas won't just make our government more representative of the diversity of our country; it will drive a political agenda that meets the needs of more people and fits the uniqueness of local communities. Positive Politics is about inspiring many people like you to get started now.

## THE MOST COMMON JOBS PEOPLE HAVE BEFORE BECOMING MEMBERS OF CONGRESS[42]

- **Public servant:** 80 percent of the House and 82 percent of the Senate served as local, state, or federal elected officials or public servants before joining Congress.
- **Lawyer:** 30 percent of the House and 51 percent of the Senate have practiced law.
- **Business leader:** 136 members were owners, founders, or executives of companies.

- **Educator:** 101 members previously worked in education, including teachers, professors, counselors, and coaches.

But a wide range of other careers are represented, including thirty-one farmers, twenty-nine marketing professionals, twenty-four nonprofit executives, twenty physicians, sixteen judges, nine engineers, and five pro athletes. To paraphrase a key quote from the movie *Ratatouille*, "Not everyone can become a great politician. But a great politician can come from anywhere." If you have a vision for solving the world's biggest problems, you're an ambitious optimist and we need you in our politics now.

### FROM SKILLS TO GREATNESS

- When he was seventeen, Alexander Hamilton wrote a letter about a hurricane so poignant that it was published in a local newspaper. This led to people in his hometown crowdfunding his move to America and his education in New York.[43] At twenty, Hamilton joined a local volunteer militia, where he gained military experience. Two years later, he had earned enough respect to be named chief staff aide to then forty-five-year-old George Washington. Hamilton was a key military advisor and drafted many of Washington's letters.
- Thomas Jefferson was a practicing lawyer from 1768 to 1773 and a state house representative before being tasked with writing the Declaration of Independence in 1776, at the age of thirty-three. As one of the youngest delegates to the Continental Congress, he was chosen not for his rank but rather for his writing ability. Jefferson went on to become governor of Virginia, secretary of state, vice president, and president.

- Benjamin Franklin led multiple careers as a scientist, inventor, author, and publisher before first being elected councilman at forty-two. In 1748, at the age of forty-one, Franklin sold half of his publishing business to his foreman, David Hall, for £1,000 per year for eighteen years, equivalent to over $4 million total in current value.[44] Now free to work on anything, Franklin dedicated the last forty-two years of his life to politics, becoming one of America's leading Founding Fathers.

## POLITICS IS EASIER THAN YOU MIGHT THINK

I've shared many examples of how Positive Politics has worked recently and over the course of American history, including both famous and lesser-known stories, to encourage you to remember that you don't need to look a certain way or have a lot of money or experience to enter politics. You already have the skills you need to succeed in politics.

As Steve Jobs said, "Life can be much broader once you discover one simple fact, and that is everything around you that you call 'life' was made up by people that were no smarter than you... You can change it, you can mold it...the most important thing...is to shake off this erroneous notion that life is there and you're just going to live in it, versus embrace it, change it, improve it, make your mark upon it... Once you learn that, you'll never be the same again."[45]

Everything we call politics is managed by a surprisingly small group of people. And you can call those people, write to those people, influence those people, become one of those people.

**CHANGE YOUR LIFE AND CHANGE THE WORLD**

Taking positive political action can transform you into an even more driven and optimistic person. You have the desire to change the world and the ability to work toward a vision for more than ten years. Apply this power to politics. Find the issues you think are most important and start fighting for these fundamental solutions in politics. Fixing these problems locally and nationally will help many more people succeed. Changing lives in this way can be your highest calling and change your life too.

## CHAPTER 5

★ ★ ★

# WHY FIGHT?

# 5.1

FIGHT FOR THE
FUNDAMENTALS

*"The test of our progress is not whether we add more to the abundance of those who have much; it is whether we provide enough for those who have too little."*

—FRANKLIN D. ROOSEVELT, SECOND INAUGURAL ADDRESS, 1937

When has politics made you feel happiest, saddest, and angriest? For me, all of these happened on one chilly, overcast Thursday evening in Coldwater, Michigan, during my first year volunteering for a political campaign.

I met a woman who ran up to us to tell us her story. She was a single mom working sixty hours per week for $8.50 an hour at Taco Bell and Wendy's just to make ends meet. She was burnt out from work but couldn't even take a few days off after working these long hours for years. She also spent nearly every waking hour outside of work taking care of her kids and her mother.

This woman from Coldwater doesn't want to be a millionaire. She doesn't want to be rich or famous. She simply needs help covering the fundamentals of her life—affordable childcare for her kids, Social Security and Medicare for her mom, a higher minimum wage at her job, and more housing in her hometown.

When we measure whether presidents and other politicians are successful, too often we focus on the biggest numbers, like whether the stock market or national debt is going up or down. But the most important numbers in our economic system are usually the smallest ones, like the minimum wage or the interest rate on a new home.

The more we focus on these fundamentals in our politics—education, healthcare, jobs, and housing—the more progress we'll actually make in America because these are direct investments in American families that will free us all up to solve bigger problems for ourselves, our families, and our country.

## WE NEED TO HELP PEOPLE THRIVE—NOT JUST SURVIVE

Treading water near the poverty line is a tough life. True freedom is having your needs met and still having the time and energy to pursue your life's calling. Democratizing this freedom will unlock the world's hidden ambition.

Abundance is key to this mission. The last two hundred years of progress pulled most of the world's population over the poverty line. The next hundred years is about lifting everyone above the abundance line. In many ways, this abundance is already here, especially with global access to technology and especially the internet. But as science fiction author William Gibson said, "The future is already here—it's just not very evenly distributed."[46] The biggest promises of technology—to provide abundant food, energy, housing, education, and medicine—are still limited to the global elite. Positive Politics seeks to democratize this abundance.

Positive Politicians need to get wins quickly and think long term to deliver on these promises. To do so, they need to use the power of the government. Increasing the federal minimum wage requires just one bill in Congress. A diverse set of states, including Florida, Oklahoma, Vermont, and Wisconsin, already offer universal pre-K.[47] And we already have public and private infrastructure in rural and urban areas throughout America to provide Medicare for all. We need to fight to increase government investments in all of these areas.

We also need our government to get back to building public housing and infrastructure. In 1998 Congress passed the Faircloth Amendment to limit US public housing development, and as a result, the number of new public housing units per year dropped from 1.4 million in 1994 to 835,000 in 2022.[48] Meanwhile, China built more than five million units of public housing from 2022 to 2023.[49] Decades of diverging levels of trust in these governments has led to US home ownership of just 65 percent, including 45 percent for millennials, while Chinese home ownership is approaching 90 percent.[50] Fixing these issues means fighting to repeal laws that limit our government's power to build.

## FIGHT FOR THESE FIVE FUNDAMENTALS FIRST

1. **Jobs:** Raise the minimum wage above the cost of living for one individual working forty hours per week and tie future increases to inflation.
   - Bill: Higher Wages for American Workers Act—Raise the federal minimum wage to fifteen dollars per hour and adjust it annually based on the rate of inflation.
2. **Housing:** Expand supply of new public housing units that our local, state, and federal governments build each year.
   - Bill: Homes Act—Establish a national housing development authority to acquire and develop affordable housing and finance local housing authorities to do the same.
3. **Education:** Fund the expansion of public schools to educate all children and adults from preschool through college.
   - Bill: Universal Prekindergarten and Early Childhood Education Act—Provide funding to expand all public elementary schools to care for preschool children.
4. **Healthcare:** Fund new public health clinics to provide preventative and curative healthcare to all Americans.
   - Bill: Medicare for All Act—Create a national health insurance program available to any American with no costs other than prescription drugs.
5. **Transparency:** Change campaign finance laws to require disclosure of large individual and corporate political contributions to fight corruption.
   - Bill: DISCLOSE Act—Require federal disclosure of the original source of any political spending over $10,000 in an election cycle.

How would these bills affect the woman from Coldwater? A $15 minimum wage would mean she could earn the same amount in just thirty-four hours per week versus sixty hours per week at $8.50. She could use that extra twenty-six hours per week to spend more time with her family and take a little time off, and when she wanted to, she could make a little more money than she does now. One bill in Congress would change the lives of everyone in her family.

## WE NEED A NEW MOVEMENT TO TAKE BACK POLITICAL POWER FOR THE PEOPLE

This means ending partisan control of elections and returning independence to our politics so our government can truly be by the people and for the people. And we must fight for open access to capital and good jobs so everyone can succeed. This is the America we deserve.

I met the woman from Coldwater almost ten years ago, in my very first year volunteering for a political campaign. My conversation with her haunted me in a positive way, leaving a core memory that will always inform how and why I take political action.

To help her and so many other Americans succeed, Positive Politicians need to focus on the fundamentals of government service, providing better jobs, housing, education, healthcare, and transparency. These are meta-solutions—solutions that create solutions. When more Americans have more time and less stress, they will use this freedom to make life better for themselves, their families, and their communities.

We need to focus on the key levers of individual opportunity—education, healthcare, jobs, and housing—and give everyone more time and resources to figure out the rest. And we need transparency so we can trust our government to efficiently provide these services to all. These five fundamentals all help to drive positive political cycles, as we discussed in Chapter 1.

## POSITIVE POLITICS SHARES KEY MISSIONS WITH OTHER RISING MOVEMENTS

Books like *Utopia for Realists*, *Abundance*, and *Public Citizens* also argue that solving the fundamentals like jobs, housing, and transparency can make the future better for all. Where these books largely sought to influence the existing political and intellectual elite, I am writing *Positive Politics* to target a new generation of leaders and recruit people like you into politics.

### RECOMMENDED READING

These books explore different fundamentals of what we should be fighting for. They elaborate on solutions that will help make more people free to create the Good Future.

- *Who Is Government?* (2025), by Michael Lewis, focuses on the positive work that government workers are already doing through federal agencies.
- *Abundance* (2025), by Ezra Klein and Derek Thompson, focuses on housing, infrastructure, and climate change.
- *Public Citizens* (2021), by Paul Sabin, focuses on making government more efficient so we can provide more services.
- *One Billion Americans* (2020), by Matthew Yglesias, focuses on immigration, housing, and education.

- *Utopia for Realists* (2014), by Rutger Bregman, focuses on jobs, universal income, and immigration.

  Once you learn why and how to fight for Positive Politics from this book, I recommend reading these books to focus on the specific issues you want to address first in your political career.

## WHAT WOULD THAT WOMAN FROM COLDWATER WANT?

More time with her family. The freedom to succeed.

That's the American Dream. Let's make it a reality for all.

When more Americans are free to succeed, we'll invent the Good Future of our dreams!

**5.2**

★

# FIGHT FOR THE AMERICAN DREAM

*"The best way to predict the future is to create it."*

—PETER DRUCKER

## WHAT IS THE AMERICAN DREAM?

In a word, the American Dream is opportunity.

The opportunity for a better life, the opportunity to succeed based on ability and effort, the opportunity to make our children's lives better than our own.

This is the dream that drew my parents more than twelve thousand miles from their land of birth to this land of opportunity. The American Dream is simply the freedom to succeed.

This is not the Hollywood dream of sports cars and private

jets. This is the Middle America dream of a starter home, two used cars, three kids, a town with good public schools, and—if you save up—just enough money for a vacation or two.

It's now popular to denigrate the American Dream. Whether it's Bernie Sanders saying "the American Dream has become a nightmare" or Donald Trump saying "the American Dream is dead," cynicism now drives our public political discourse.

That's reflected in Americans' satisfaction ratings, which have now been below 50 percent for the way things are going in the US for more than twenty straight years.[51]

**Combined Satisfaction with Way Things Are Going in US and in Personal Life**

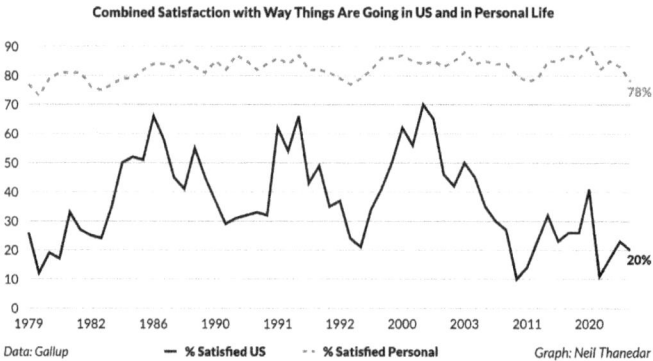

Data: Gallup    — % Satisfied US    - - % Satisfied Personal    Graph: Neil Thanedar

Source: Frank Newport, Gallup, 2024[52]

But when I talk privately to friends, family, and neighbors, left, right, and center, I frequently hear a desire to reclaim that classic American optimism and focus on what we can do to improve our communities and country.

The American Dream has always been about getting a fair chance to build a happy family life: anyone who works hard should be able to own their own home, start their own business, and control their own destiny.

The American Dream is a fundamentally optimistic vision for the future—it's the idea that all that's needed for a better life is hard work. This self-determination is essential both personally, because those who believe they control their own destiny are more successful, and politically, because our social and economic systems should be designed to directly align work and success. We need to re-center the American Dream both culturally and politically in this new era.

Positive Politics means fighting for our original optimistic vision of the American Dream and focusing on how we can maximize each person's chances for success. And it means organizing our politics around positive-sum actions, like bills that prioritize all citizens.

The American Dream relies on the same principles as Positive Politics: we need to be nice, take action, get wins quickly, think long term, go direct, and be independent. Or more simply, do the work and spread the word.

## POLITICAL MOVEMENTS AREN'T FORCES OF NATURE—THEY'RE CREATED BY PEOPLE

Positive Politics won't just happen. We need to organize a movement of people, activists, and politicians who will fight for these fundamentals. And the best time to start is now.

You don't need to quit your job and run for president now. You don't even need to run for office ever. But you can start advocating for a bill today. Or volunteer for a local candidate. Or create a new community nonprofit. You can commit one hour a week or one hundred. The details don't matter now. Just get in the game.

We all need a positive agenda that quickly improves lives and reverses the decline of the American Dream in the last fifty-plus years. Since the 1970s, real wages have stagnated, manufacturing jobs have declined, infrastructure has aged, and healthcare and education have gotten more expensive.[53] This has caused income inequality to rise and trust in our government to fall. Positive Politics can reverse these trends and restore the American Dream for all.

## THE FALL AND RISE OF INCOME INEQUALITY

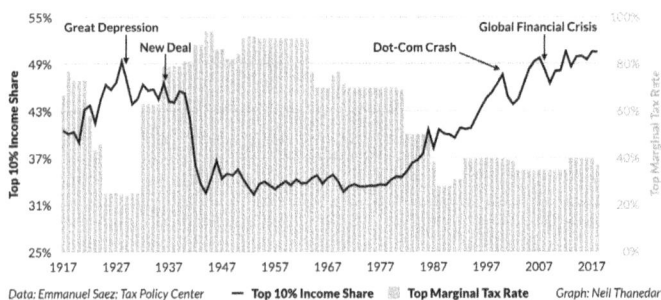

Data: Emmanuel Saez: Tax Policy Center  — Top 10% Income Share    Top Marginal Tax Rate    Graph: Neil Thanedar

Source: Emmanuel Saez, 2020[54]; Tax Policy Center, 2023[55]

## HOW DO WE GET BACK TO THE AMERICAN DREAM?

Let's go back to first principles. "Life, liberty, and the pursuit of happiness" is a good place to start. Our government was built to protect these inalienable rights. But America has failed to live up to these promises throughout our history.

We owe it to ourselves and future generations to finally complete this vision. This means reconciling our political tensions and unifying as Americans. This means rising above partisan conflict that subverts the power of the people. And this means finally addressing economic unfairness that rewards elites at our expense. Chapter 11 covers ten specific issues that we must solve to help restore the American Dream.

This is an arduous mission that will take decades to fully complete. It will require systemic social, political, and economic change. But we must do it, because on the other side of this work is the true American Dream for all.

*"This is your home, my friend, do not be driven from it; great men have done great things here, and will again, and we can make America what America must become."*

—JAMES BALDWIN

## WHAT CAN WE LEARN FROM AMERICA'S LAST OPTIMISTIC ERA?

One key is having big missions like the Space Race and the civil rights movement to organize our energies. In 1962, John F. Kennedy said, "We choose to go to the Moon in this decade and do the other things, not because they are easy, but because they are hard; because that goal will serve to organize and measure the best of our energies and skills."[56] The March on Washington, in 1963, similarly coordinated the greatest voices of the civil rights movement into a unified movement. We lost a lot of this optimistic energy after the JFK and MLK assassinations.

We need new missions to focus our political and activism efforts now. This includes pursuing policies that create an abundance of resources so we can provide more universal services, like education and healthcare, and improve the quality and availability of jobs and housing. And it means thinking long term and building a future with a more democratic American Dream for all.

## POSITIVE POLITICS IS HOW WE GET TO THE GOOD FUTURE

We don't get the future of our dreams. We get the future that we build. If we want the Good Future, we have to fight for it. So it's worth clearly defining the Good Future.

## THERE ARE TWO VERSIONS OF THE FUTURE

- **The Bad Future**, described in shows like *Black Mirror*, is the realistic-to-cynical take on where the world is going.
- **The Good Future**, presented in shows like *Star Trek*, is the realistic-to-optimistic take on where the world is going.

## IT'S EASY TO BE CYNICAL

You might think that we're living in the Bad Future now. But I still believe in the Good Future. The future with abundant resources and opportunities for all. The future where humanity becomes a multiplanetary species and Earth is carefully preserved as our home planet.

There are many people who profit from the idea of the Bad Future: Politicians who need polarization to raise money and rally their base. Corporations that sell us the tools of our own destruction. Online influencers who gain clicks and ad revenue from farming outrage.

We should celebrate great works of fiction and nonfiction that envision the Good Future. Even *Star Trek* movies have become more dystopian since 2009. Books and movies like *The Martian* and even TV shows like *Ted Lasso* demonstrate the public desire to think positively about our present and future. Artists can support Positive Politics by creating optimistic stories and images that inspire us to keep fighting for the Good Future.

### THE GOOD FUTURE NEEDS ITS OWN LEADERS

Most importantly, we need more new people like you in our politics—ambitious optimists who believe in the Good Future and are ready to fight for Positive Politics. All of us together are the Positive Politics movement.

We need to organize. We need to fight back. We need to be reformers, not just rebels. Positive Politics is how we get good things done. The Good Future is why we fight. Positive Politics is how we fight. The Good Future is the vision. Positive Politics is the mission.

### GET STARTED NOW

The following chapters will present my playbook on how to get politically active and do it in a positive way. We need new policies, but we need new politicians even more. That's why the rest of this book will focus on how to get into politics and get things done. Once you start taking political action, you'll find there are many positive paths to progress. Find your highest purpose through politics and get started now. Let's get to work!

# PART II

★

# HOW

CHAPTER 6

★ ★ ★

# HOW TO GET STARTED

## 6.1

✦

# START WITH ACTIVISM

*"Either write something worth reading or do something worth writing."*

—BENJAMIN FRANKLIN

On November 10, 2016, Katie Fahey, a twenty-seven-year-old from Michigan, published a one-sentence Facebook post asking if anyone was interested in fighting gerrymandering.

**Katie Rogala Fahey**
November 10, 2016 · 🌐

I'd like to take on gerrymandering in Michigan, if you're interested in doing this as well, please let me know ☺

Source: Riley Beggin, Bridge Michigan, 2018[57]

This turned into a Facebook group, which turned into a nonprofit organization, Voters Not Politicians, which collected over 400,000 signatures to get Proposal 2 on the ballot in Michigan in 2018. On November 6, 2018, less than two years after Fahey's Facebook post, over 2.5 million people (61.3 percent) voted to make Proposal 2 a constitutional amendment. This created an independent redistricting commission in Michigan, replacing the old system where partisan state legislatures drew the maps for their own districts. Michigan is now one of only seven states with an independent commission setting its state and congressional districts.[58]

Voters Not Politicians didn't stop with that one win. In 2022, VNP advocated for the successful Promote the Vote ballot campaign that guaranteed statewide early voting in Michigan. And in 2025, the organization joined the Michiganders for Money Out of Politics ballot proposal to add reporting requirements on groups spending unlimited amounts of money on political races and ban public utilities and major contractors from lobbying state political leaders.[59] Each of VNP's three major campaigns is an example of direct democracy, where activists collect signatures to introduce a ballot proposal and pass it with a public statewide or citywide vote. Direct democracy is a classic way to use activism to change laws and lives.

Watch the documentary *Slay the Dragon* to follow the ups and downs of Fahey's mission to end gerrymandering in Michigan, from tears of sadness over a frivolous lawsuit challenging the ballot proposal to tears of joy after winning the case and the statewide vote.

## WHY ACTIVISM?

If you want to be a politician one day, one of the best things you can do now is become an activist. The key skills you'll learn as an activist, such as networking, team-building, public speaking, and turning ideas into bills, are a great foundation for becoming a politician. There are opportunities in every city and state to focus on important issues like gerrymandering and use activism to fix things quickly. This experience will teach you how to influence public opinion and make positive change. And once you see the impact of your direct activism, you'll want to do more and bigger things in politics. We'll discuss this more in Chapter 7.

Activism is the gateway into politics. Many of our most successful modern world leaders, including Nelson Mandela in South Africa, Barack Obama in America, Aung San Suu Kyi in Myanmar, and Lech Walesa in Poland, started in activism before reaching the highest levels of politics. Activism is often a faster path to impact than running for politics first and will give you valuable experience before you get into office.

The hardest part of politics is getting started. This book highlights simple ways to start small in activism and still make a difference in politics. Theodore Roosevelt said of politics, "Start with the little, and do not expect to accomplish anything without an effort." Just start.

## HOW TO BECOME AN ACTIVIST

You don't need permission to be an activist. You can start now. You might already be an activist. If you've ever attended a march, called a local politician, or signed a petition, you've taken steps toward activism. But there's more you can do to make a difference.

Activism works best with a precise mission, dedicated team, and relentless work:

1. Pick a specific issue that you want to fix.
2. Find out who's already working on a solution.
3. Reach out to them directly and offer to help.
4. If no organization exists, create it yourself.
5. Drive toward that mission for years.

Focus on one issue, even one bill, and rally support from your friends and neighbors before expanding. It doesn't have to be a major national effort; local is often better. Since local politics is much less polarized than national politics (66 percent of Americans have a favorable opinion of local government, while just 32 percent have a favorable opinion of the federal government), it can be easier to build consensus locally first.[60] Taking any political action will change you, inspire you, and drive you to make further change.

Through activism, you'll learn which issues can only be solved at specific levels of government. For example, problems with housing and public schools are best handled at the local level. Improvements in education standards and healthcare regulations usually start at the state level. And issues like immigration, national defense, and international relations must be tackled at the national level. By building your activism experience from local to national, you'll have the full range of options to get stuff done as a politician. We'll discuss this more in Chapter 7.

Organizing is key to activism and politics. Find the individuals and enterprises working on your mission and join them. If you can't find any groups coordinating this work, start connecting with activists and create events and organizations yourself—then use this political power to start changing laws and improving our world. We'll discuss this more in Chapter 8.

## STARTING SMALL IN ACTIVISM

*"Politics ought to be the part-time profession of every citizen who would protect the rights and privileges of free people."*

—DWIGHT D. EISENHOWER

You can also start with activism while still in your first career. People often imagine politics and activism to be high-stakes, all-or-nothing, lifetime commitments. But the reality is that we're all already active in politics; it's just a matter of degree. For too many of us, our only political engagement is at the ballot box or on social media. Get out into your community; attend local town halls, community associations, and party meetings; and join political organizations that align with your values. Take small actions now so you can take bigger actions later.

The key is starting where you're comfortable and expanding your engagement over time. If you're an introvert, standing on stages, giving passionate speeches, and running for office may seem scary. But you can organize rallies, write speeches, and run campaigns behind the scenes too. Remember, there are twenty-four competitive Oscar categories, and only four go to acting. Just like a movie cannot be made without a director, screenwriter, production designer, sound engineer, editor, and more, campaigns need a manager, communications director, legal counsel, fundraisers, organizers, and advisors. If you're not ready to be in front of the camera now, start behind the camera.

## MAKING POLITICS YOUR SECOND, THIRD, OR FOURTH CAREER

I want to inspire more successful professionals to get into politics by starting with activism and being "multisport athletes" for their whole lives. Startup founders and other high performers make great activists and politicians because abilities like setting a vision, building teams, raising funds, scaling operations, and chasing a mission are also how successful activism movements and political campaigns are run. The skills you've built through your education and experience are exactly what our politics needs. You're more prepared for politics than you may think.

You don't have to run for office (or donate millions) to make a difference in politics. Just pick one issue you love and advocate for it. Start local. If you're not ready to run, help someone you know run. Find other politicians who support your issues and support their next campaign. Let's focus on the fundamentals and solve America's biggest problems.

## 6.2

☆

# FIND YOUR ISSUES

*"Politics is too serious a matter to be left to the politicians."*

—CHARLES DE GAULLE

I believe the most important issue in politics today is campaign finance reform. Solving the money problem in politics will simultaneously fix most of our problems with negative campaigning, lobbying, corruption, and waste.

If we wanted politics to be as negative as possible, what would we do? We would allow anyone in the world to secretly spend unlimited money on our elections. Most of that money would go toward negative advertising, especially against new, independent-minded candidates. The rest would go toward lobbying and other legalized forms of corruption. The only winners would be establishment politicians, large corporations, and foreign governments.

It's not a coincidence that we had the most positive presidential campaign of the last twenty years in 2008, right before the 2010 *Citizens United v. FEC* Supreme Court ruling, which legalized unlimited dark money spending in our elections. Before 2010, this type of political contributions was illegal, with state laws like the Michigan Campaign Finance Act of 1976 and federal laws like the Bipartisan Campaign Reform Act of 2002 restricting political spending. The Citizens United ruling reversed decades of state and federal campaign finance reform.

Dark money is political spending by groups that do not disclose their donors, and it's rapidly taking over our political system: such spending amounted to $1.9 billion in the 2024 election cycle, up from $144 million in the 2010 election cycle.[61] We need new bills and amendments to ban dark money and require political candidates and organizations to disclose all of their donors. Finally finishing the fight for campaign finance reform is a meta-solution that will make our politics more transparent and enable journalists and citizens to follow the money and measure its influence.

Campaign finance reform is my number one issue in politics. I'm now executive director of the Michigan Campaign Finance Network, leading investigations into dark money in Michigan politics. Every story I break adds transparency to our politics and makes open government bills and amendments more likely to be passed in Michigan. We'll discuss this more in section 11.2.

## WRITING IS AN IMPORTANT WAY TO IMPACT PUBLIC OPINION AND LAWS

Henry George started his career as a teenager working on a ship sailing to India before he headed to California to attempt gold prospecting, failed, and became a journalist in San Francisco.[62]

His most famous writing, the 1879 book *Progress and Poverty*, sold millions of copies and inspired a movement called Georgism, which focused on taxing economic value not created by the owner, a concept called economic "rent."[63] By taxing economic rents like the value of land, we could increase revenues from this unearned income and lower taxes on earned income. Henry George went on to place ahead of Theodore Roosevelt in the 1886 New York City mayoral election.[64] George's fight for equality of opportunity still influences America's progressive, democratic, and reform-minded activists who seek to help more people succeed, as we discussed in Chapter 5.

## FOCUS ON META-SOLUTIONS TO MAKE THE MOST IMPACT IN POLITICS

Meta-solutions are solutions that create more solutions. Campaign finance reform is one of these meta-solutions in Positive Politics. But there are many other ways to fix our politics and government to help create more solutions.

Making our government more transparent is a classic meta-solution. The Freedom of Information Act (FOIA), passed unanimously by Congress in 1966, requires disclosure of government documents upon request. However, federal and state government entities often make FOIA requests difficult, redacting key information, delaying replies for months to years, exempting specific lawmakers from these disclosures, and charging high fees to provide this information. Passing more open freedom of information laws would allow journalists and the public to audit their own government and push politicians to do the right thing transparently.

Making our government more efficient is also an important meta-solution. The more we trust our government to spend our tax dollars efficiently, the more willing we will be to vote to provide more fundamental government services for all. Positive Politicians should focus on delivering government services efficiently so we can earn the right to do more good.

## WHAT ARE THE FUNDAMENTAL ISSUES IN POLITICS NOW?

As discussed in section 5.1, five fundamental issues affect every American every day. The following are my key proposals to address these issues:

1. **Jobs:** Create more training and funding so people can get better jobs and start their own businesses. Forty hours per week should cover a family of four.
2. **Housing:** Build millions of new homes and apartments so housing is affordable for all, on a single income. Make moving to cities and centers of opportunity easier.
3. **Education:** Ensure free pre-K through college for every American. This is an investment that will pay off in all future generations, especially for our children.
4. **Healthcare:** Provide universal healthcare so every American is covered and healthcare is no longer tied to employment. This will also collectively save us over $1 trillion per year.
5. **Transparency:** Require all political contributions be publicly disclosed and easily trackable to minimize corruption in government and help more people get into politics.

Go to any town hall in America and you will hear these five issues above all else. Why? Because these are all key meta-solutions to life's problems. Solving these problems for every American is more than a safety net; it's a trampoline helping people rise up. Reclaiming the American Dream means making succeeding as easy as possible for everyone.

Issues like public safety, environmental protection, and social security come up frequently and should be part of the Positive Politics agenda too. The common feature of all of these issues is that they provide upward mobility and help people help themselves. Over 66 percent of Americans believe the federal government has the responsibility to provide these social services for all Americans.[65] The more we focus on the fundamental meta-solutions of politics, the greater the long-term positive impact we'll have on America.

## FOCUS ON ISSUES, NOT PERSONALITIES

Are you not yet comfortable engaging politically under your own name? Use a pen name. I expect the future of campaigning to be like the politics in the book *Ender's Game*, where aspiring leaders pseudonymously debate online to influence governments and people globally.

Pseudonymity, which has a long history of being used in politics, can also be supercharged by the internet. Alexander Hamilton, James Madison, and John Jay wrote the Federalist Papers using the shared pseudonym "Publius." Benjamin Franklin used multiple pseudonyms, including Silence Dogood, to share his social commentary. There is even evidence of Roman graffiti in places like Pompeii that anonymously campaigned for specific politicians. There is power in this secrecy, especially when the opponent is a vengeful authoritarian.

Imagine a future in which presidential candidates are known only by their usernames and avatars. You might see a pink dragon and a yellow honey badger debating in virtual reality, surrounded by millions of fans on each side, with their voices intentionally anonymized and androgenized to prevent bias, and artificial intelligence (AI) fact-checking each candidate in real time. This might seem straight out of science fiction, but I think we'll start to see elections with pseudonymous candidates by 2050.

Pseudonymity is great for Positive Politics because it keeps the focus on ideas, which are easier to judge neutrally, instead of on politicians, who are easy to attack personally. And pseudonymous politicians can always go public later, like our Founding Fathers did. But even with technology, politics will still come down to the same basic principles: making promises and keeping them. Your ideas will make the most positive impact when you get real stuff done.

## IT DOESN'T MATTER HOW YOU GET STARTED—JUST DO IT

Activism is the most direct path to making a positive impact in politics. So if you want to get into politics, start with activism. Pick a specific issue that you want to fix and focus on getting stuff done in this area before expanding. Focus on metasolutions to have the most positive impact. The next chapter explains how to take direct action in politics and organize collective action to scale this work.

# CHAPTER 7

⭐ ⭐ ⭐

# HOW TO GET STUFF DONE

# 7.1

☆

# TAKE DIRECT ACTION

*"In any nonviolent campaign, there are four basic steps, collection of the facts to determine whether injustices are alive, negotiation, self-purification, and direct action."*

—MARTIN LUTHER KING JR.

In 1982, Gregory Watson, a nineteen-year-old sophomore at the University of Texas, learned that there was a congressional pay amendment that had been approved by Congress with the ten amendments of the Bill of Rights but was never fully ratified by the states in 1791.

Watson wrote a paper for his government class arguing that this amendment should finally be ratified. After receiving a C grade on the paper, he led a nationwide campaign to complete this ratification, which was finally certified in 1992 after 30 new state legislatures voted to approve the amendment.

In 2017, the University of Texas officially updated Gregory Watson's student record to change his grade from a C to an A+, stating, "In light of the student's heroic efforts to prove the professor and TA wrong in their assessment of his term paper, Mr. Watson deserves A+."[66]

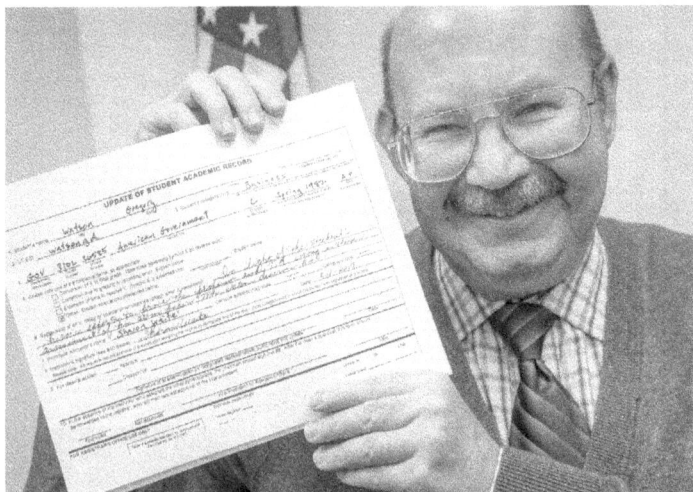

Gregory Watson with his Update of Student Academic Record application.
Source: Jay Janner, Austin American-Statesman, 2018[67]

## WHY DIRECT ACTION MATTERS

Imagine a world where Gregory Watson just accepted his C and never pursued this idea. Our Constitution would be shorter. The financial and political incentives in Congress would be worse. But because Watson turned his idea into direct action through activism and politics, our government is improved.

Ideas by themselves don't hold much weight in politics. Anyone can shout "impeach the president" online or in the streets, and nothing will happen. But if you call one congressman willing to draft articles of impeachment and rally a team of friends and volunteers to call their members of Congress to cosponsor the bill, an impeachment vote could happen in Congress within a week. The same is true for any popular bill. Rallying support and directing it at a focused cause is one of the fastest ways to make a positive impact in politics.

One great example of direct action is how a group of bipartisan bloggers got the US Senate to end a secret hold and vote on a bill to make all federal grants and contracts transparent. In 2006, Senators Barack Obama and John McCain cosponsored the Federal Funding Accountability and Transparency Act of 2006, a bill to create a public, searchable database of all federal grants and contracts. When two other senators used a parliamentary procedure to secretly hold this bill to prevent it from coming to a vote, both left-leaning blogs like *TPMmuckraker* and right-leaning blogs like *GOPProgress* advocated for readers to call their senators to identify the blockers.[68]

Over the next twenty-four hours, ninety-six senators publicly denied holding the bill, which led the two senators blocking it to identify themselves and remove the hold. This bill, which eventually passed unanimously in the Senate, led to the creation of USAspending.gov, which many government officials, journalists, and individuals use to track and audit government spending. Fast, positive political action is possible when we all work together publicly.

### WHAT YOU CAN GET DONE IN POLITICS

Gregory Watson's heroic activism took a decade and resulted in one of only twenty-seven constitutional amendments in American history. It's amazing to think about what you could get done in politics in one decade. But that time frame can also feel daunting, so I want to focus now on the opposite—what can you get done through activism in one day, one hour, or even one minute?

**TIME TO ACCOMPLISH KEY ACTIVISM GOALS**

| TIME FRAME | PLAN | ACTION | IMPACT |
|---|---|---|---|
| One Minute | Call your member of Congress. | Tell them how to vote on your favorite bill. | Calls influence representatives more immediately than voting. |
| One Hour | Speak at a public meeting in support of your favorite issue. | Prepare a concise statement and passionately deliver it live. | Public comments are often broadcast locally and popular messages can go viral online. |
| One Day | Write a blog post advocating for your favorite bill. | Send the link to your representative and share it online. | Links are easy to share among representatives and well-argued blog posts can change their minds and votes. |
| One Week | Create a local petition about a specific city council issue. | Write a one-page explainer to share with the council, the media, and your neighbors. | Get your city council to focus on the public instead of special interests. |
| One Month | Get one or more bills passed at the city, state, or federal level. | Educate yourself on new bills. Pick one and take direct action. | Gain an understanding of the political process from idea to bill and learn how to identify and avoid blockers. |
| One Quarter | Register one hundred voters. Collect one thousand signatures for a ballot proposal. | Print forms, get a clipboard, and talk to people at the busiest intersections. | Talk to your neighbors and learn what they really think about politics. |

**TIME TO ACCOMPLISH KEY ACTIVISM GOALS**

| TIME FRAME | PLAN | ACTION | IMPACT |
|---|---|---|---|
| One Year | Join a nonprofit. Get elected to your local school board or city council. | Search for nonprofit jobs. Find out when the next local elections in your district are. | Make politics your full-time job. Change laws one bill at a time. |
| One Term | Build your political team. Pass ten or more bills. Grow your audience. | Join committees. Introduce new legislation. Meet as many representatives as possible. | Be a true representative for all people and lead your governing body. |
| One Decade | Earn political capital. Win statewide or national office. | Collaborate with other Positive Politicians to take direct action. | Build a record of lifesaving legislation. Change the world! |

## START TAKING DIRECT ACTION NOW

What can you do today to take direct action in politics? Go beyond the list above and think about what issue you most want to impact first. Is this a local, state, or federal problem? Who is closest to solving this problem now? Challenge yourself to take at least one concrete action today, and see how it changes your life and the world.

## 7.2

☆

# TURN YOUR IDEAS INTO BILLS

*"Our right to alter our government must be used to sweep these halls clean of greedy interests so that people may use this government in service to each other's needs and to protect the condition of our earth."*

—DORIS HADDOCK

Doris "Granny D" Haddock lived from 1910 to 2010—one hundred years, one month, and thirteen days to be exact. The first fifty years of her life were happy but private, with a long marriage, kids, grandkids, and twenty years in one job. But that quiet life changed in 1960, when the fifty-year-old Haddock started her activism career by organizing tea parties to protest Project Chariot, a proposal to test nuclear weapons off the shore of Alaska. Haddock's activism led to the signing of the Partial Test Ban Treaty in 1962, an international agreement banning nuclear weapons tests in the air, space, or water.[69] We're all still benefiting from the international politics inspired by Haddock's activism to slow the nuclear arms race.

This kick-started a fifty-year career in activism and politics for Haddock. She is most famous for walking from Los Angeles to Washington, DC, at eighty-eight to ninety years old, to advocate for campaign finance reform. This 3,200 mile walk, during which Haddock averaged ten miles per day for fourteen months straight, ended on February 29, 2000; the Bipartisan Campaign Reform Act passed just two years later.[70] This bill, commonly called the McCain–Feingold Act, added transparency rules like "Stand By Your Ad," which states that political ads have to announce who paid for them. Haddock had left her lasting mark on politics again.

Granny D was not afraid of standing up to power. After arriving in Washington, DC, at the end of her cross-country walk, she kept protesting around the capital for months. On April 21, 2000, she was arrested along with thirty-one other activists for reading the Declaration of Independence inside the US Capitol Building. In her court statement that May, she said, "In my ninety years, this is the first time I have been arrested... But, Your Honor, some of us do not have much power, except to put our bodies in the way of an injustice—to picket, to walk, or to just stand in the way. It will not change the world overnight, but it is all we can do."[71]

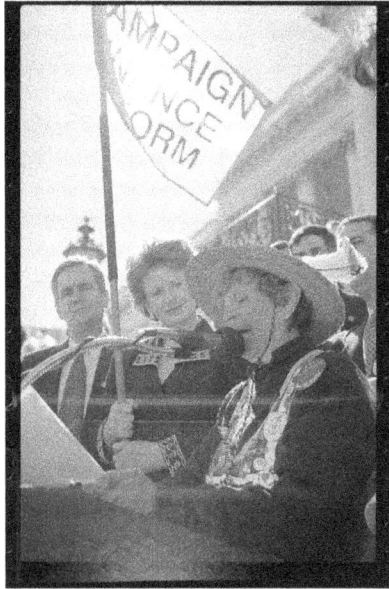

Doris "Granny D" Haddock speaking outside the US Capitol in 2000 after her cross-country walk advocating for campaign finance reform.
Source: Tom Williams, Library of Congress, 2000[72]

Doris Haddock's story closely fits our Positive Politics playbook. She started with activism, taking direct action and focusing from the beginning on turning big ideas into bills. In 2009, she founded the nonprofit Open Democracy and continued her fight for campaign finance reform throughout her life. At ninety-four years old, she even ran for US Senate. She also celebrated her ninety-eighth, ninety-ninth, and hundredth birthdays working at the New Hampshire State House.[73] Most politicians could build their whole legacy around passing even one of these huge bills. Seeing how Haddock made positive change in state, federal, and international politics, all in the second half of her life, is awe-inspiring. Doris 'Granny D' Haddock is a powerful example of how Positive Politics can create an amazing life and change the world.

Watch the documentary *Run Granny Run* to follow the ups and downs of the last four months of Doris Haddock's 2004 campaign for US Senate.

## LONG BEFORE A BILL BECOMES A LAW, IT'S AN IDEA IN AN ACTIVIST'S HEAD

Some ideas are already popular. For example, over 80 percent of Americans want the government to be able to negotiate with pharmaceutical companies to lower medication prices. Getting an idea like this into a bill is as simple as convincing one member of Congress to write it and two or more members from each party to cosponsor it.

Other ideas take time to build popular support. In 1996, just 27 percent of Americans supported same-sex marriages. That number rose to 71 percent by 2022.[74] Activism organizations fought publicly for decades to improve popular support for LGBTQ+ issues. This is incredibly important work that must be done before ideas can become bills.

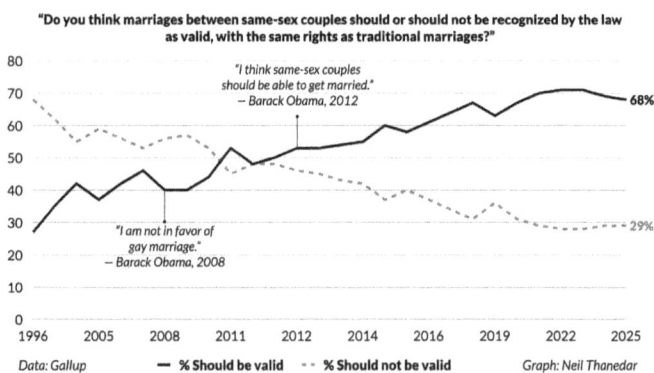

**"Do you think marriages between same-sex couples should or should not be recognized by the law as valid, with the same rights as traditional marriages?"**

*"I think same-sex couples should be able to get married." — Barack Obama, 2012*

*"I am not in favor of gay marriage." — Barack Obama, 2008*

| Data: Gallup | — % Should be valid | - - % Should not be valid | Graph: Neil Thanedar |

Source: Gallup, 2024[75]

One of the best ways to get involved in politics in a nonpartisan way is to advocate for a specific bill to be passed. In 2023, I wrote a blog post titled "End Accredited Investor Laws" in which I explained how these restrictions block 90 percent of Americans from accessing the best startup investments. One day earlier, H.R. 2797, the Equal Opportunity for All Investors Act, had been introduced in the House. One month later, H.R. 2797 passed the House 383–18. My blog post, calls, and emails helped secure Democratic cosponsorship for this bill.

## ACTIVISM VERSUS POLITICS

Activists turn ideas into bills. Politicians turn bills into laws.

- If an issue has greater than 50 percent popular support and isn't a law yet, that's a politics problem.
- If an issue has less than 50 percent popular support, that's an activism problem.

Few politicians will introduce a bill that they know is not supported by the majority of their constituents, because they know every such move hurts their next election.

It's the job of activists to change that popular support through sustained attention, support, and direct action, which forces politicians to change their views.

This idea is called the Overton window, a concept created by Joseph Overton at the Mackinac Center for Public Policy in Michigan to explain the range of policies that politicians can support while still being popular enough to win elections. After Overton's death in 2003, his friend and colleague Joseph Lehman coined and popularized the term.[76]

Politicians operate within the Overton window. It's activists' job to shift this range. As Lehman said, "The most common misconception is that lawmakers themselves are in the business of shifting the Overton window. That is absolutely false. Lawmakers are actually in the business of detecting where the window is, and then moving to be in accordance with it."[77]

## OVERTON WINDOW SHIFT ON
## SAME-SEX MARRIAGE: 1996–2023

| OVERTON WINDOW 1996 | OVERTON WINDOW 2011 | OVERTON WINDOW 2023 |
|---|---|---|
| 27% FOR 68% AGAINST SAME-SEX MARRIAGE | 48% FOR 48% AGAINST SAME-SEX MARRIAGE | 71% FOR 28% AGAINST SAME-SEX MARRIAGE |
| Bill Clinton signed the Defense of Marriage Act on September 21, 1996, defining marriage as a legal union between one man and one woman. | Barack Obama, 2008: "I am not in favor of gay marriage." Barack Obama, 2012: "I think same-sex couples should be able to get married." | Joe Biden signed the Respect for Marriage Act on December 13, 2022, requiring all US states and territories to recognize same-sex marriages. |

DISAPPROVE OF SAME-SEX MARRIAGE  ←  →  APPROVE OF SAME-SEX MARRIAGE

Source: Becky Bowers, PolitiFact, 2012[78]

Over long periods of time, the Overton window tends to shift slowly from conservative to progressive. But these shifts are punctuated by periods of extreme change, like the civil rights movement of the 1960s and the modern LGBTQ+ rights movement.

These changes don't just happen automatically. Activists use all forms of media—including movies, music, and books—and all forms of action—such as protests, negotiations, and boycotts—to push the acceptable range of political discourse forward. The best politicians work with activists to identify new policies that are gaining widespread support and turn those ideas into laws.

## ACTIVISM MAKES IMPORTANT ISSUES POPULAR

Let's say you want to increase legal immigration to the United States. You have an activism problem, because only 26 percent of Americans currently support this issue. Thirty-eight percent want immigration to stay the same, and 30 percent want it decreased.[79]

## AMERICAN IMMIGRATION TRENDS: 1965–2025

"Thinking now about immigrants (that is, people who come from other countries to live here in the United States), in your view, should immigration be kept at its present level, increased or decreased?"

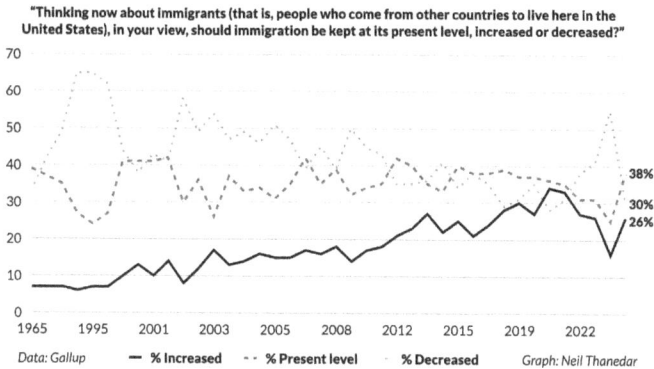

Data: Gallup    — % Increased    - - % Present level    % Decreased    Graph: Neil Thanedar

Source: Lydia Saad, Gallup, 2025[80]

But you may know many great stories of immigrants who struggled for years to come to America and then thrived, became creators, employed numerous Americans, and made their communities stronger. Effective activism here can be as simple as publicly telling these stories, one tweet or blog post at a time.

It's easy to have a fear of the unknown. Authoritarian politicians often use fear of crime and chaos in distant cities to stoke anger and resentment locally. For example, even though the

US violent crime rate decreased 49 percent from 1993 to 2019, 78 percent of Americans believed that crime was going up in the US.[81] Interestingly, only 38 percent of these people thought that crime was going up in their area.[82] This gap between local and national knowledge demonstrates that we're in a constant battle to get the facts right.

## POLITICS TURNS POPULAR ISSUES INTO LAWS

Now let's say you want to pass a congressional stock trading ban. That's a political problem. You have the public on your side, but not the politicians. Eighty-six percent of Americans, including 87 percent of Republicans, 88 percent of Democrats, and 81 percent of independents already favor "a proposal to prohibit Members of Congress and the family that lives with them from trading stocks in individual companies."[83] So why hasn't this bill passed already? Because members of Congress are the people who write and pass our bills. As long as the public is distracted with other issues, politicians will continue to block bills that hurt them or their donors.

Find a way to show politicians how many people are on your side. Polls are a great way to focus media and public attention on the popularity of an issue and force politicians to respond. This is one key strategy that think tanks use to drive specific legislation. Most politicians won't change their votes until the public gets involved. So the only solution is to get loud. Write. Speak. March. Protest. Coin a phrase. Make petitions. Organize rallies. Convince thousands of people to post online, send emails, and call their representatives. Get celebrities to call out politicians on social media. There is strength in numbers.

Positive Politicians can ride these public waves of activism to quickly change laws. The net neutrality movement that started in 2017 is a great example of this public strategy. After the FCC announced plans to repeal net neutrality rules, advocates for a free and open internet succeeded in rallying millions of citizens, plus celebrities, influencers, and major tech companies, to voice support and join protests. In 2024, the FCC officially restored net neutrality. Public pressure organized by activists is a powerful forcing function for politicians.

Once you have public support, recruit your cosponsors. Find a few leaders in each party who will publicly support the movement early and have them call their colleagues to rally votes. A 2022 study analyzing forty years of congressional data found that "Representatives and Senators who are able to attract a significant portion of cosponsors to their bills from members of the opposite party are more successful at advancing their bills through the legislative process. This is true for both minority *and* majority party members and across a large range of political conditions."[84] Bipartisanship is key to getting laws passed.

### PASSING BILLS CHANGES THE WORLD

When we take action, get wins quickly, and think long term, we can make our politics and government more effective, which positively benefits us all. At the end of a long political career, no one will remember how many total bills you passed. But they will cite the one to five biggest bills you got passed, so find issues that can positively change the world. We'll discuss this more in Chapter 10.

Earning a reputation for writing, advocating for, and changing laws is how you build power in activism and politics. You can start building this power yourself, but the greatest strength comes from organizing collective action. We'll discuss this more in Chapter 8.

★ ★ ★

# HOW TO BUILD POWER

## 8.1

☆

# EARN POLITICAL CAPITAL

*"Why political power? Because it shapes all of our lives. It shapes your life in ways that you might never think about. Every time a young man goes to college on a federal education bill passed by Lyndon Johnson, that's political power. And so is a young man dying in Vietnam. Every time an elderly person is able to afford an MRI, that's Medicare. That's political power."*

—ROBERT CARO

### YOU CAN EITHER BUY, BORROW, OR EARN POWER

In business, this concept is simple. You can become CEO by acquiring a business, being hired by a business, or founding a business. Buy, borrow, or earn.

There's a mythology around earned power. In business, Steve Jobs's return to Apple in 1997 is an example of the story of the prodigal son. When a founding CEO refers to "our company" or "us," it holds more power than when such references are made by a hired CEO. And the love goes both ways. As a three-time founding CEO and father of three, I know enough to say that I truly have a parental bond with my startups, even after they've grown up and moved out.

In his book *Great Founder Theory*, Samo Burja compares "borrowed vs. owned power," obviously favoring owned power. But earned power is much more valuable and durable than bought power, even though both are owned power. Earned power doesn't need to be defended as carefully because for someone to beat you, they have to earn it too. This is another way in which those with earned power can be more independent.

## IN POLITICS, YOU BUY, BORROW, AND EARN POWER DIFFERENTLY

Corporations and their lobbyists buy power through campaign contributions and "independent" expenditures. Most of the federal government is run by employees with borrowed power who use their titles and budgets to get stuff done until the next administration comes in and replaces them with their own people.

Truly earned power is rare in politics. We see it when leaders like MLK create new movements. We see it in America's Founding Fathers, most of whom went directly from fighting the Revolutionary War to fighting to keep our new country together through interstate disputes and internal rebellion. And we see it in the presidents who led us through each major Fourth Turning crisis: George Washington during the Revolutionary War, Abraham Lincoln during the Civil War, and FDR during World War II. Earning power is obviously the best. Borrowing power is obviously the worst. And buying power is fast but fleeting.

## THE TWO KEYS TO EARNING POWER ARE TO
## START EARLY AND STAY INDEPENDENT

Buying or borrowing power is a shortcut to the top, but this can be a deal with the devil in which you trade your long-term independence for short-term success. Starting early with activism is a powerful way to earn power, especially if you build strong networks and organizations to lead your movement. And building independent income streams, like books, podcasts, events, and subscriptions, can give you the freedom to pursue politics full time. Content creators can use this route to earn power with their audiences that they can use to positively impact activism and politics.

You don't have to be a millionaire or billionaire to be independent. In fact, many of the world's richest people operate almost entirely on borrowed power. Think about the hedge fund managers and venture capitalists who invest other people's money or the corporations and startups that are funded by those investors. They rely on their ability to leverage resources that aren't theirs. It's better to make five to six figures independently than to make seven to ten-plus figures working for the man, especially if you want real earned power.

### WHAT IS POLITICAL CAPITAL?

In his 1961 book *Political Influence*, political scientist Edward Banfield introduced the idea of "political capital," a "stock of influence" earned, saved, and spent by politicians. There are many ways to earn this capital, from influencing voters, to winning elections, to gaining seniority and leadership positions. This kind of power is hard to win and easy to lose, but those who hold it can direct entire branches of government.

Money can buy political capital, but it's not an efficient conversion. Especially since the 2010 *Citizens United v. FEC* decision by the US Supreme Court, which allows corporations and other organizations to make unlimited independent political expenditures, running for federal office requires millions of dollars. And of the sixty-five candidates who spent over $1 million of their own money to run in congressional or presidential elections, only ten won.[85]

Media skills like knowing how to earn views, subscribers, and members online will be increasingly valuable in politics as debates and organizing moves online. Activists can organize large movements to use their combined political capital to trigger more significant change, and politicians can speak directly to their own audiences, making it easier to be independent. By combining multiple sources of political capital, you can build political power at any time. You may already have more political capital than you think.

### THE TWO PATHS TO POLITICAL POWER

There are both insider and outsider paths into politics. Each of these paths has multiple lanes, some windier than others.

On the insider path, you can start in the candidate lane, working your way up from local elections to larger races. You can also rise up through the campaign lane, going from volunteer to staffer to director to campaign manager. The ultimate insider lane is the party lane, where you can start attending local county party meetings and rise to party chair before running for office. This is the route Nancy Pelosi took in California starting in the 1960s; she was first elected to Congress in 1987.

The outsider path has become more defined since Donald Trump won two presidential elections. Building power and winning elections as an outsider requires a portfolio of skills. The top three outsider lanes are business, finance, and media. Experience in business demonstrates the ability to build personal wealth. Experience in finance demonstrates the ability to raise and leverage other people's money. And experience in media demonstrates the ability to win and hold an audience. The best outsider politicians are masters of all three.

This power can also be wielded from far outside politics. Throughout his career, Elon Musk has built immense business wealth and financial leverage, which he used to buy Twitter (now X). This media control plus the ability to spend over $200 million of his own money through campaigns and PACs (political action committees) in the 2024 election alone made Musk the most influential nonpolitician in the second Trump presidency.

The best leaders build power both inside and outside elected office. Two current congresswomen, Nancy Pelosi and Alexandria Ocasio-Cortez, each rose to the top of a faction of the Democratic party by first supporting other politicians and then running themselves and building coalitions inside Congress.

Nancy Pelosi worked her way up from volunteer to state party chair over the 1960s and 1970s before winning her first congressional election in 1987. In Congress, she used her fundraising skills to support Democratic politicians nationwide and rose from minority whip to minority leader to Speaker of the House by refusing to follow seniority customs and whipping votes in the whole House Democratic Caucus. Pelosi has maintained her power after stepping down as House Democratic leader in 2022, even whipping votes for committee leadership in 2024 while in a hospital bed recovering from a fall and having her hip replaced.[86] Nancy Pelosi represents the power of controlling the Democratic party from the inside out.

Read *The Art of Power* by Nancy Pelosi for more on her rise to power.

Alexandria Ocasio-Cortez (AOC) worked as an organizer on Bernie Sanders's 2016 presidential campaign before launching her first congressional campaign in 2017. Ocasio-Cortez continues to build power directly with people while in Congress, speaking transparently to her more than twelve million Twitter followers and more than eight million Instagram followers with videos and messages that clearly explain how committees work, which bills need support, and why she votes in specific ways. She's also an influential member of the Congressional Progressive Caucus (CPC) and setting herself up for a long career as a Democratic leader. AOC has demonstrated the ability to organize power through the public from the outside in.

Watch *Knock Down the House* for more on AOC's rise to power.

### START BUILDING YOUR POLITICAL POWER NOW

Voting is the simplest thing you can do to impact politics. But it's just one signal every few months or years, and one that is highly diluted, especially in national elections. Organizing, campaigning, protesting, educating, writing, petitioning, fundraising, striking, and boycotting are all great ways to be more politically active. By consistently taking direct action to turn ideas into laws, you can build a successful career as a Positive Politician and change the world.

# 8.2

*

# ORGANIZE COLLECTIVE ACTION

*"From the depth of need and despair, people can work together, can organize themselves to solve their own problems and fill their own needs with dignity and strength."*

—CESAR CHAVEZ

In 1985, twenty-five politically active women met in the basement of activist Ellen Malcolm's home. Their mission was to elect more female Democratic pro-choice politicians. At that time, no Democratic woman had ever been elected to the US Senate in her own right, and the Democratic party focused its money and support on incumbent male politicians. But Malcolm believed that if the organization raised early money for rising female politicians, they could seed these candidates' success and help them raise more money later. They dubbed this idea Early Money Is Like Yeast (because "it makes the dough rise"), and EMILYs List was born.[87]

The number of women in Congress has since skyrocketed, starting in 1986 when early support from EMILYs List helped elect Barbara Mikulski to the US Senate. EMILYs List has now helped elect 175 US congresswomen and more than 1,500 women to state and local office.[88]

## WOMEN IN CONGRESS: 1917–2023

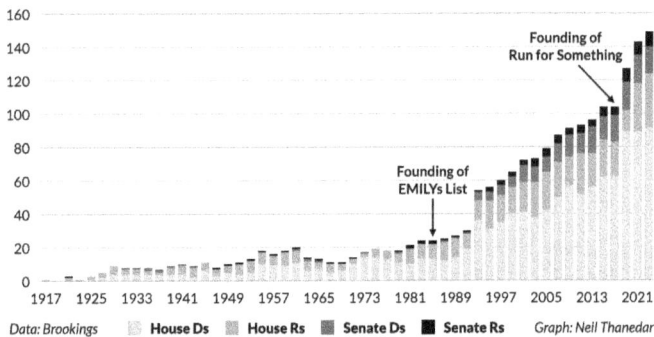

Source: Molly E. Reynolds and Naomi Maehr, Brookings, 2024[89]

## BUNDLING PEOPLE AND MONEY

The EMILYs List strategy of bundling small donations from hundreds of thousands of members is so effective that even competing organizations—like Susan B. Anthony Pro-Life America, which raises money for female candidates who oppose abortion—use this model to fundraise and organize for their causes.[90] Why does it work so well? It's easy to focus on the money, but the greatest power is the list. When a new candidate or issue arises, activism groups with large communities can quickly mobilize to take action. And politicians who rise up through these organizations together can enter office with a network of people they know and trust to work together and get stuff done. We'll discuss this more in section 9.2.

Organizing large groups of passionate activists is a powerful form of potential energy in politics. We should use this power to rally our Positive Politics community to take more political action and elect candidates who support our mission. The most direct way for us to launch new candidates is through a Positive Politics accelerator, where we can bundle early money, advice, and support for many new Positive Politicians each year. This model can support both new activists and new politicians. We'll discuss this more in section 11.1.

Read *When Women Win* by Ellen Malcolm and Craig Unger to learn about Malcolm's origin story and follow the ups and downs of EMILYs List's biggest races.

## NEW TOOLS FOR ORGANIZING

Activists also use all modern resources available to them. We're long overdue for the greatest tech and media minds to use their online skills to positively influence politics. Barack Obama used the internet to advertise and organize for his campaigns, and Donald Trump used podcasts and social networks to share his ideas, but this is just scratching the surface of the power of online organizing. New technologies like AR (augmented reality) and VR (virtual reality) can help political candidates directly reach their constituents and build rapport with other politicians.

This is good news for a new, positive trend in politics. When US Representative Alexandria Ocasio-Cortez livestreamed her congressional orientation on Instagram, she didn't just share political knowledge—she made us feel like insiders. Her direct, unfiltered approach has inspired a new generation of political communicators who understand that authenticity beats artifice. The best Positive Politicians make the public feel like part of their team.

Social media has effectively amplified protests in many countries, from the Occupy movement to the Arab Spring to Gezi Park. While protests effectively focus public attention on important problems, these movements have failed to maintain that energy to advocate for specific positive reforms. The first civil rights movement to use social media to focus on solutions while organizing political power will find immense leverage to positively reform our politics.

## POSITIVE VERSUS NEGATIVE FEEDBACK LOOPS IN POLITICS

Every day, more than eleven thousand federal lobbyists wake up and get to work seeking to influence the 535 members of Congress.[91] That's more than twenty lobbyists for every congressperson. You might actually agree with some of these lobbyists. For example, nonprofits like the National Resources Defense Council (NRDC) lobby to advocate for pro-environment policies like clean air and water for all. And for over one hundred years, the NAACP has famously used both lobbying and litigation to advance civil rights in America that benefit us all. So not all lobbying is necessarily bad.

But the vast majority of lobbying, thirty-four times that of any other category, goes to support "business and industry."[92] This includes defense contractors lobbying members of the House and Senate Armed Services Committees, banks and hedge funds lobbying Financial Services Committee members, and many industries lobbying Appropriations Committee members to create loopholes and subsidies from Congress. This special-interest lobbying is largely net negative for America, since a few corporations and billionaires usually benefit massively while we all pay more money for fewer public goods and services.

## THE NEGATIVE FEEDBACK LOOP IN POLITICS

1. Moneyed interests lobby politicians to enact negative-sum policies that benefit them.
2. Our government provides fewer goods and services while increasing taxes and debt.
3. The big money lobbies to privatize more government services for their benefit.
4. Our government provides fewer goods and services while increasing taxes and debt.

But there is a better way. Positive Politicians need to build momentum for our movement by passing good laws quickly while pushing toward our long-term positive-sum mission. For example, Social Democrats like Victor Berger in Wisconsin were positively labeled "Sewer Socialists" for focusing on tangible quality-of-life improvements like new sanitation systems, which earned them the right to make bigger government reforms like fighting corruption and graft. Berger was the first socialist elected to the US Congress and focused on government efficiency reforms during his four terms.[93] As we discussed in Chapter 5, by focusing on fundamental issues, we can deliver bigger positive-sum reforms that benefit everyone.

### THE POSITIVE FEEDBACK LOOP IN POLITICS

1. Positive Politicians enact positive-sum policies that benefit all Americans.
2. Our government provides more goods and services while decreasing taxes and debt.
3. The public majority votes to elect more Positive Politicians ready to do this work.
4. Our government provides more goods and services while decreasing taxes and debt.

By publicly proving that politics can make everyone's lives better, Positive Politicians will earn the right to do more good with our government. Driving more positive feedback loops in politics is how we build power for the Positive Politics movement.

### NEGATIVE VERSUS POSITIVE FEEDBACK LOOPS IN POLITICS

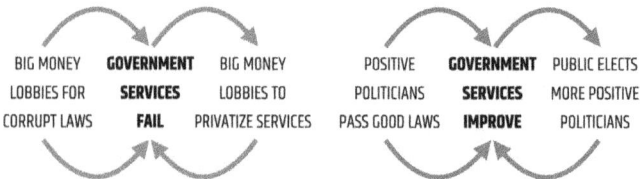

| BIG MONEY LOBBIES FOR CORRUPT LAWS | **GOVERNMENT SERVICES FAIL** | BIG MONEY LOBBIES TO PRIVATIZE SERVICES | POSITIVE POLITICIANS PASS GOOD LAWS | **GOVERNMENT SERVICES IMPROVE** | PUBLIC ELECTS MORE POSITIVE POLITICIANS |

## CREATING A MOVEMENT

For maximum political power, turn your issue into a movement. While the term "civil rights" has been used in the English language for over four hundred years, the 13th and 14th amendments made these rights a key focus of our politics.[94] And it took abolitionist senators like Lyman Trumbull and Charles Sumner, who authored the original Civil Rights Acts of 1866 and 1875, to push Abraham Lincoln from within their own party to more aggressively fight slavery and transition our country from the Civil War to the civil rights movement.[95]

We can't just win; we have to do it the right way. The best civil rights leaders fight from the moral high ground. We always have a responsibility to resist unjust laws and leaders. But it's not enough for the ends to justify the means; a saying often credited to Mohandas Gandhi warns us that "an eye for an eye leaves the whole world blind." From the March on Washington led by Martin Luther King Jr. in 1963 to the Salt March led by Gandhi in 1930 to the Boston Tea Party in 1773 to the entry of Jesus into Jerusalem on Palm Sunday in approximately AD 30, the long history of social movements proves that you don't need weapons to win. Modern social movements like the LGBTQ+ rights movement peacefully advocated for the nationwide legalization of same-sex marriages through the Supreme Court's *Obergefell v. Hodges* decision in 2015. Positive Politicians can learn successful strategies from all of these movements.

Positive Politics is how we organize a movement that can get wins quickly and succeed over the long term at changing the world. We need more ambitious optimists like you in our activism and politics now. The next great positive nonviolent movement needs leaders. Get ready to run your first race and build your political team in the next chapter.

# CHAPTER 9

★ ★ ★

# HOW TO WIN ELECTIONS

## 9.1

☆

# RUN YOUR OWN RACE

*"A politician thinks of the next election. A statesman, of the next generation."*

—JAMES FREEMAN CLARKE

In 64 BC, Marcus Tullius Cicero was running for consul, the highest public office in the Roman Republic. He was an outsider, and no non-noble man had become consul in over thirty years at that point. But Marcus climbed the ranks of Roman society, getting a great education, doing military service, working in legal defense, and serving in the offices of quaestor and praetor. Still, to reach the highest office, he had to run the perfect race. So his younger brother, Quintus Tullius Cicero, Marcus's loyal advisor, wrote a pamphlet explaining how to run the campaign. This text, now translated into the book *How to Win an Election*, has survived over two thousand years, and its strategies closely match how we run campaigns today.

The fundamentals of winning elections haven't changed. As Quintus wrote, "Running for office can be divided into two kinds of activity: securing the support of your friends and winning over the general public." Ensuring your family, friends, and close network actively support your campaign is essential for your early energy and focus. This group is where you'll usually find your first volunteers and funds. In local races, you can win whole elections with just this small team. But even national races require a lot of personal support that's best given by people who truly care about you. We'll discuss this more in section 9.2.

Marcus did win the race for consul. Two years later, Quintus was elected praetor, and he later served as a Roman governor. Their strategies were obviously successful two millennia ago. Why does this playbook still work today? Because politics hasn't changed much. Our systems are more democratic, now ensuring one vote per person almost universally. But the fundamentals haven't changed. Do good work outside politics, then work your way up from local to national offices, solving key problems for people the whole time. This is how you consistently win in politics.

Read *How to Win an Election* by Quintus Tullius Cicero to see how little has changed in politics over the last two-thousand-plus years. The even pages are in the original Latin, the odd pages are in English, and the main text is just eighty-four small pages.

## FINDING THE RIGHT RACE FOR YOU

If you get into politics expecting to run for president right away, you're going to have a bad time. The presidency is at the very end of a long journey from activism to politics. I'm not here to promise you a ten-year path to the presidency. Even if that's what you want, there are so many other factors, from timing to luck to charisma, that are beyond the scope of this book.

But if you're willing to start at the bottom in politics and work your way to the top, this book and especially this chapter are for you. In the Roman Republic, this ladder of success was called *cursus honorum* (Latin for "course of honors"). In that culture, you were expected to serve in the military, courts, and administrative state before being eligible for higher offices.

There is a similar expectation in America today. As we discussed in Chapter 2, the number one previous career for members of Congress is public service. Lawyer is number two, and business is number three. But members of Congress who held positions as local, state, or federal public servants outnumber those who held any other job. Learn to serve in smaller roles and you'll truly earn the right to hold higher office.

Starting small also makes your first race more manageable. In a state representative's district with ninety thousand residents, about fifteen thousand people will vote in a primary election and thirty thousand will vote in a general election. Three people each knocking on one hundred doors per day can reach every single primary voter in less than two months. Local races are even smaller. In a city with eight thousand residents, you could win a mayoral election with one thousand votes. Too many people decide they want to become runners, immediately sign up for a full marathon, and promptly quit. Don't make the same mistake in politics. Find a race that fits your current skills and resources.

## BUILDING YOUR PUBLIC BASE

Once you've built your internal support, you can start expanding your public support. "This is done by knowing who people are, being personable and generous, promoting yourself, being available, and never giving up,"[96] per Quintus's advice. This fits closely with the Positive Politics principles "be nice," "get wins quickly," "go direct," and "think long term." It's not enough to do the work; you also have to let people know what you've done. The public wants a direct connection to their politicians, and social media scales this ability to go direct.

"Knowing who people are" also mirrors my section 5.1 call to fight for the fundamentals. Politics is a game of who can promise and deliver the most of what people want. Positive Politicians who follow through on their promises to improve quality of life and successfully promote their progress will win elections on the power of their public bases. In other words, do the work and spread the word.

## IF YOU LOSE, KEEP RUNNING

Quintus's advice to never give up brings me back to advising my dad's first campaigns. We did a few things right and a lot of things wrong in that first election in 2018. Establishment politicians and reporters were skeptical of Shri Thanedar, but most everyone he met in person liked him and loved that he was different from the average politician. His accent went from a problem to an opportunity, with our TV ads showing Michiganders humorously struggling to pronounce our last name and my dad helping them with a smile. He started building a base as a populist underdog.

After months of work, we finally started making progress. My dad rose in the polls from 2 percent to 30 percent in the first half of the campaign, winning two statewide polls in March versus the establishment favorite, Gretchen Whitmer. The attacks started in April, and he eventually dropped to 18 percent and lost the race. While he struggled to get over 10 percent in rural Michigan, he convincingly won cities like Detroit and Flint. I drove the whole I-75 corridor from Flint to Detroit with my brother on election day, stopping at every polling location we could find. The energy was incredible. People desperately wanted someone new in their politics.

Unlike a lot of outsider candidates who run once, lose, and quit, we got started immediately on our next race. For 2020, we set our sights much lower, at a state representative seat. Instead of being the sole governor representing all ten million Michiganders, my dad would be one of 110 representatives. But we had a clear focus: his home district—District 3—north Detroit from 8 Mile to 6 Mile and Livernois to Gratiot—an area that voted for Shri for governor by over 50 percent in many precincts. In two short years, we had gone from massive underdog to serious favorite.

## WINNING YOUR FIRST ELECTION

Everything you learn in your first election, especially if it's a loss, will make you better in future campaigns. We came into our first race with business skills—fundraising, marketing, communications, operations. Now we had the political skills too—polling, mapping, messaging, canvassing. We executed a simple, positive, issues-focused campaign that talked to every voter and won the primary election by 15 percent and the general election by 89 percent in an open safe seat. At about 2:00 a.m. on August 5, 2020, we knew we had won. Nearly four years of daily work had led to this major success!

Once you win your first race, you'll find that bigger opportunities open up to you as well. Each step up is like another first election because you're talking to many new voters. In our case, an open seat for US Congress became available in 2022, so we immediately got to work again to run for this higher office. Even with over $6 million in PAC spending against him in the last five weeks of our primary campaign, my dad won this primary election by 5 percent and the general election by 49 percent. He won reelection in 2024 and is now a two-term US Congressman. Positive Politics really works!

## HOW TO KEEP WINNING

Politics is still a popularity contest. Like Quintus said, "The most important part of your campaign is to bring hope to people and a feeling of goodwill toward you."[97] That's easy to do once but harder to do repeatedly. Once you win your first race and get into government, you have to deliver on as many of your promises as possible, but you can't do this all yourself. That's why building your perfect team is such a crucial piece of winning elections.

## 9.2

☆

# BUILD YOUR POLITICAL TEAMS

*"A house divided against itself cannot stand."*

—ABRAHAM LINCOLN, ILLINOIS REPUBLICAN
STATE CONVENTION, 1858

In 1860, four men were running for the Republican nomination for president of the United States. The frontrunner was New York Senator William Seward. Also running were Ohio Governor Salmon Chase, former Missouri Attorney General Edward Bates, and former US representative from Illinois Abraham Lincoln. You know who won.

Afterward, Lincoln named all three of his Republican presidential opponents to his cabinet, with William Seward as secretary of state, Salmon Chase as secretary of the treasury, and Edward Bates as attorney general. This "Team of Rivals" helped win the Civil War and created a better future for America.

Read *Team of Rivals* by Doris Kearns Goodwin to learn more about the teamwork in Lincoln's cabinet from 1861 to 1865 during the Civil War.

You never win in politics by yourself. Even if you're running for local office and managing the whole campaign yourself, you're always being supported by your family and friends, the unsung heroes of politics. From there, you need to recruit a professional team to run your campaigns and another team to run your office. And once you really start to earn political power, you can build alliances, squads, caucuses, and even new parties to organize collective action in government. Start building your political dream team now.

## 1. RALLY YOUR KITCHEN CABINET

Every US president has an official cabinet, a group of leaders who each manage a department of the executive branch. These people are also supposed to be the president's closest advisors. But it usually doesn't work that way. In reality, presidents and other politicians tend to have an even tighter group of advisors, which can include family members and people who have worked with the candidate for years. This inner circle is now called a "kitchen cabinet."

Politicians tend to trust their inner circle more than their official teams. Andrew Jackson learned this lesson the hard way. In 1831, Jackson found himself in conflict with Vice President John Calhoun and members of his cabinet who were loyal to Calhoun.

So he increasingly relied on his close team of advisors, which became known during his presidency as his "Kitchen Cabinet."[98] This strategy can be criticized for putting too much power outside official government positions, but kitchen cabinets provide key stability to politicians, especially in times of crisis. You should already be thinking about who would be in your kitchen cabinet.

Kitchen cabinet members can hold multiple roles simultaneously. Eleanor Roosevelt served as both First Lady and her husband Franklin Roosevelt's closest advisor. Robert F. Kennedy served as attorney general while he was in his brother John F. Kennedy's kitchen cabinet. And Teddy Roosevelt had a "Tennis Cabinet" of friends and advisors from inside and outside government who met with the president nearly daily, played tennis, and discussed policy. Find your kitchen cabinet and tell them you want to get into politics now.

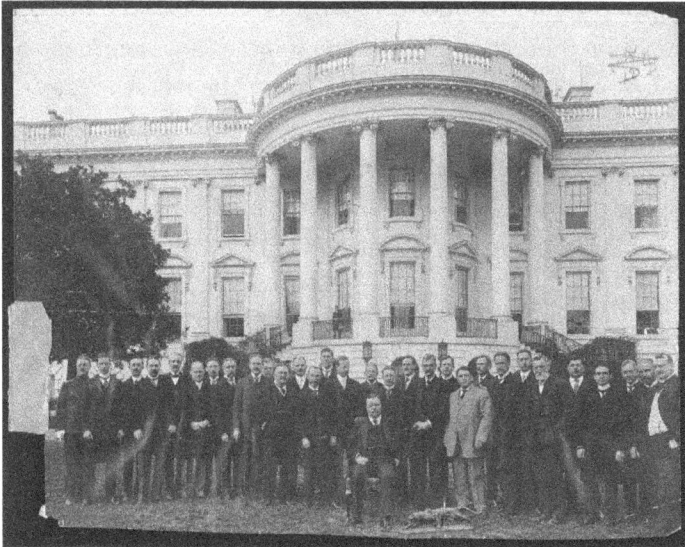

President Roosevelt and his Tennis Cabinet
Source: Barnett M. Clinedinst, Library of Congress, 1909[99]

## 2. FIND YOUR TOP LIEUTENANTS

The two most important roles in any political team are the chief of staff and the communications director. The chief of staff is usually the operational leader of the campaign, like a COO in a startup supporting the candidate as CEO. I've also seen successful campaigns where the chief of staff is the CEO. As a political advisor once told me, "The candidate isn't the quarterback; they're the football!" And the communications director is usually the other public face of the campaign, responsible for working with the media and public to get your message out clearly. These two individuals are like the co-founders of your campaign, so hire wisely.

The next two important leaders are your field director and your finance director. Depending on how much money you can raise and spend, you can either focus on an "air" attack, where you take big shots on TV and radio ads and mailers, or execute a strong "ground" game, where your organizers and volunteers knock on thousands of doors to promote your campaign one person at a time. Obviously, the bigger the race, the easier it is to reach large numbers of voters through the air, and that makes your finance director even more important. You, as the candidate, can fill one or more of these roles yourself, as long as you save enough time to actually run for office.

## 3. RECRUIT YOUR POLITICAL STAFF

Once you win your first election, you'll need at least two professional teams: one to manage your current office and another to run your next campaign. There's always another campaign.

## THERE ARE AT LEAST THREE KEY FUNCTIONS YOU NEED TO RUN ANY PROFESSIONAL POLITICAL TEAM

1. Communications: How you talk to the public through media
2. Field: How you meet voters in person
3. Finance: How you raise money to run your operations and pay your team

You'll also need to do operational, legal, and administrative work, a lot of which can be handled by contractors, volunteers, and interns. Again, you can run some or all of these teams yourself in smaller races. But you will supercharge your campaigns if you can find great leaders and contributors for each of these functions and then let them hire their own teams. Always remember that you, the candidate, are ultimately responsible for wins and losses. Like Harry Truman would say, the buck stops with you as the leader.

As is the case with startups, every person you hire increases your burn rate. The average congressional office spends 76.2 percent of their budget on personnel.[100] Some hires can help you fundraise and decrease this burn rate. But you should be very aware of how your team affects your runway. When campaigns go into debt, that financial responsibility can linger for decades: Senator John Glenn ran for president in 1984 and didn't finish paying off his debt until 2007.[101] So make sure your team always fits your budget.

## 4. BUILD COALITIONS ACROSS PARTIES AND BRANCHES

Once you've built your own political team, it's important to start networking with other politicians and their teams to see whom you can work with on different bills. Be open-minded here. Your cosponsors could be from a faraway state or even a different party.

A great way to network with other politicians is to organize issue-aligned alliances and caucuses. There are hundreds of caucuses in Congress, like the Fix Congress Caucus and the Friends of Bulgaria Caucus. You can make your own caucuses focused on anything. Let's make a Positive Politics Caucus!

You can start building these alliances even before you win your first race. Democratic groups like Run for Something and Justice Democrats, Republican groups like Moms for Liberty and American Majority, and independent groups like With Honor and New Politics all work to support candidates and help them win early races. Positive Politics can do the same with our accelerator and community. We'll discuss this more in section 11.1.

## USE YOUR TEAM'S POWER TO POSITIVELY CHANGE THE WORLD

By being independent, going direct, and thinking long term, you can build trust across the political spectrum and maximize your ability to change laws. The power you earn by building great political teams and alliances gives you leverage to positively change the world. Positive Politics can be a powerful alliance we can use to reclaim the American Dream and invent the Good Future. As we decided in Chapter 5, this is why we fight. Let's go change the world.

# CHAPTER 10

★ ★ ★

# HOW TO CHANGE THE WORLD

**10.1**

☆

# USE YOUR BULLY PULPIT

*"I suppose my critics will call that preaching, but I have got such a bully pulpit!"*

—THEODORE ROOSEVELT

A pulpit is the podium where a preacher speaks. A century ago, when Teddy Roosevelt coined the term "bully pulpit," people used the word "bully" like we use the word "awesome" now. So a bully pulpit basically means an amazing platform to change hearts and minds.

Roosevelt believed that the US presidency was the biggest bully pulpit in the world, and he proudly used this power to influence public opinion to support his progressive reforms. He especially focused on giving the media more access to the government, inviting journalists to travel with him on trains during his trips around the country and becoming the first president to create a press room in the White House. We can all use our bully pulpits to change the world.

## YOU DON'T NEED TO BE A POLITICIAN OR CELEBRITY TO HAVE A BULLY PULPIT

Being famous or having a lot of money for ads increases the breadth of your influence. But social connections can have a much deeper impact on changing minds and actions. A 2020 field experiment found that friend-to-friend texting increased voter turnout by 8.3 percent versus an increase of 0.29 percent for automated get-out-the-vote texts.[102] In-person activism with your friends can have an even bigger impact, so don't underestimate your ability to influence politics.

You already have a bully pulpit. Use it to inspire your friends and family to take positive political action. Encourage your cynical uncle who complains that all politicians are corrupt to show up and speak at your next city council meeting. He might actually enjoy getting the opportunity to talk at the podium and make his voice heard. And he'll see that both the local politicians and the attendees of these meetings are a lot like him.

Read *The Bully Pulpit* by Doris Kearns Goodwin for more on how Roosevelt pioneered the use of direct public engagement and media relations to rally public support for his agenda.

## REMEMBER WORRYING ABOUT THE
## DESTRUCTION OF THE OZONE LAYER?

In the 1970s, chemists Paul Crutzen, Mario Molina, and Frank Sherwood Rowland identified that nitric oxide (NO) and chlorofluorocarbons (CFCs) were causing ozone loss. Molina and Rowland published their paper in June 1974 and testified before the House of Representatives in December 1974. Congress funded the National Academy of Sciences (NAS) to confirm this ozone loss thesis, which it did, and in 1982, twenty countries, led by the United States, began meeting to form an international agreement to phase out CFCs and other ozone disruptors, culminating in the 1987 Montreal Protocol on Substances That Deplete the Ozone Layer.

Scientists identified the problem, politicians formulated the solution, and the whole world continues to reap the rewards. The ozone hole has been recovering consistently since the 1990s and is projected to return to at or above 1980s levels by 2040 around most of the world.[103] Crutzen, Molina, and Rowland received the 1995 Nobel Prize for Chemistry "for their work in atmospheric chemistry, particularly concerning the formation and decomposition of ozone." This international partnership between scientists and politicians is an excellent example of Positive Politics.


## USE YOUR POLITICAL VOICE FOR GOOD

Negative politicians use fear to get your attention. They want you to be scared because that keeps you watching them and voting for them. Local and cable news repeatedly show and debate the same murders and court cases, which makes us believe crime is going up. But crime has actually been going down consistently for over thirty years.[104] Telling the truth repeatedly with transparent data and personal stories has the power to break through the negativity and convince more people to fight for Positive Politics.

**US Violent Crime Rate and Americans' Perceptions of Crime Rate vs. Year Ago**

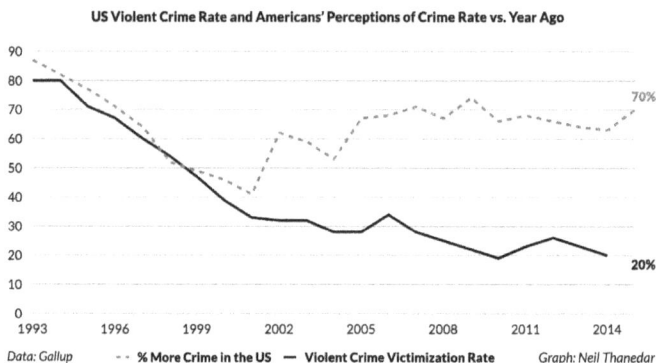

Data: Gallup    - - % More Crime in the US    — Violent Crime Victimization Rate    Graph: Neil Thanedar

Source: Justin McCarthy, Gallup, 2015[105]

Positive Politicians use facts to keep us focused on the right problems. By focusing on the fundamentals, as we discussed in Chapter 5, we can spotlight the good work done by our government and encourage the public to support us investing more in the future. Facts can overcome fear when the person at the pulpit is someone you trust.

## THE INTERNET IS HISTORY'S BIGGEST BULLY PULPIT

New online platforms are also a powerful tool to push positive messaging. "The medium is the message," Marshall McLuhan famously wrote, and nowhere is this more evident than in the transformation of modern political communication.

Mass media is organized around short segments squeezed

in between ad breaks, so the message is sanitized and shrunk to fit that space. Conversely, online streaming and social media allow for much freer and more real conversations. And critically, there's no middlemen online, so politicians can speak directly to the public. As our Positive Politics principles "go direct" and "be independent" recommend, use new media channels to talk directly to your voters and inspire them to change the world with you.

Modern media is rapidly decentralizing now. The rare, coveted position of talk show host is now open to anyone with a smartphone and an internet connection. We wield massive power in what we create and consume. Let's focus on positive people who actually get things done, not narcissists spewing fake outrage. By using the internet and other modern media to amplify positive work being done by politicians, we can rally the public to support more ambitious and optimistic government programs.

## HOW TO STAY ON MESSAGE

Paul Tully, political director for the Democratic National Committee in the 1980s and 1990s, developed a two-by-two strategy for political communications now called the Tully Message Box. Imagine a grid with four boxes: "us on us," "us on them," "them on us," and "them on them." At any given time in a political campaign, media attention is usually focused on one of these four boxes.

The best box for us is obviously "us on us." This is where we define ourselves. Our Positive Politics principles "be nice" and "be independent" both align with us staying focused on our own box as much as possible. If the media or other candidates try to get you out of your box, deflect the negativity and be relentlessly positive about your message, like we discussed in Chapter 1. It always helps to start sharing your story early, before they can attack you.

**HOW TO PLAY THE TULLY MESSAGE BOX**

| US ON THEM | US ON US |
|---|---|
| USE SPARINGLY | FOCUS HERE! |
| THEM ON THEM | THEM ON US |
| TOTALLY AVOID | PIVOT BACK |

The mass media's power to drive negative politics is waning. Network and cable television rewarded conflict and negativity because that's what worked for thirty-second ads between five-minute segments on twenty-four-hour channels. Political consultants and PACs still push attack ads because they're stuck in this outdated mindset. But most voters today, especially younger ones, get political information through social networks and other direct channels. The good news is that it's easier to stay on message when you control your own distribution.

Look at the rise of politicians like Michigan State Senator Mallory McMorrow, whose passionate speech defending herself against false attacks went viral largely through social media sharing. She didn't need a TV ad buy or a press conference—she just spoke truthfully and let the public do the rest. Her following grew from a few thousand to over 200,000 in days because she stood up for herself and brought the conversation back to her actual policy ideas. Constantly pivoting back from "them on us" to "us on us" will earn you a public reputation for positivity.

New media tools are enabling the rise of direct, social, and authentically positive political communication. The medium really is the message—and new media can reward hope over fear, solutions over attacks, and authentic positive engagement over manufactured outrage. Being positive is not just a good communications strategy; it's also a long-term winning strategy in political game theory, especially as the media changes to be more open.

## THE BEST POSITIVE CONTENT IS BOTH EDUCATIONAL AND ENTERTAINING

It's true that dramatic lies spread faster than boring truths. There are two key solutions here:

1. Simple: Tell more interesting truths.
2. Strategic: Call your shot. Tell the truth years before they lie.

Former US Representative Katie Porter's whiteboard presentations on complex policy issues routinely get millions of views because she explains solutions in a passionate and engaging way. When she breaks down healthcare costs or banking regulations, she's proving that positive, substantive content can spread faster than negative sound bites.

And it's not just about views—it's about having followers

who stay engaged and actually show up. When Representative Porter needed constituents to pressure insurance companies during the pandemic, her online community responded in force. That kind of sustained engagement simply doesn't come from negative messaging—but it *can* come when public servants focus on positive, productive problem-solving, using direct engagement with their constituents.

## USE YOUR BULLY PULPIT TO CHANGE THE WORLD

The evidence is clear: politicians who master positive communication in the social media age build more durable support than those who still rely on mass media attacks. Activists and politicians have an amazing platform from which to convince the public to be more positive and take action to change the world. The future belongs to politicians who understand how to use their bully pulpits to push our governments to take a more positive-sum approach. This is how we fix our social contract and make Positive Politics a reality.

**10.2**

✦

# FIX OUR SOCIAL CONTRACT

*"Force does not create right...we are obliged to obey only legitimate powers."*

—JEAN-JACQUES ROUSSEAU, *THE SOCIAL CONTRACT*, 1762

A country is basically a club. You join, follow rules, pay dues, and in return you get access to a specific set of benefits all in one place. This deal between a government and its citizens is a social contract, and it includes both explicit benefits like employment opportunities and access to healthcare and implicit benefits like the status of being American at home and abroad.

If your club or country starts deteriorating, or otherwise stops providing good services, you could quit, complain to management, or just quietly remain a member. These choices are called *"Exit, Voice, and Loyalty"* in Albert O. Hirschman's classic book, and they're seen as the three main responses to state decline.

But there's a fourth response to failing institutions, and that's action. You can identify the services you wish were better and get to work fixing them. If that's school lunches, first use your voice by going to your next PTA meeting and sharing plans that have worked in other districts. If they don't commit to fixing the problem, run for school board and fix it yourself. This path from voice to activism is available to all of us at every level of government.

## TRUE DEMOCRACIES REQUIRE HEALTHY
## SOCIAL CONTRACTS TO BE SUCCESSFUL

Legitimate political authority cannot come by force. It must be earned. The US Constitution begins with "We the People" in big, bold letters to signify that our government's authority is derived from all of us. The Declaration of Independence also affirms this idea of popular sovereignty, stating that "Governments are instituted among Men, deriving their just powers from the consent of the governed." The ultimate power in America resides with the people.

This principle—that political authority requires voluntary collective consent—represents the foundational promise of democratic society. This is how we balance individual freedom with collective needs. And it should be how we decide what we value most in our society. Every bill in Congress, state legislatures, and city councils amends this social contract, adding or removing funding and services. Whether our government gets better or worse every day comes down to which bills are introduced and who wins these votes. These are the front lines of our politics, where we need to fight to make our government better.

We live with our social contract every day, whether we like it or not. But internally, we're constantly judging whether this deal with our government is fair. Most Americans now lack confidence in the way their taxes are being spent by their federal government (66 percent) and their state government (58 percent).[106] It makes sense that people are unhappy with the current system. Governments are failing to live up to their end of the social contract.

## FIGHTING CORRUPTION WILL FIX OUR SOCIAL CONTRACT

Positive Politicians need to fight corruption to earn back public trust in our government. Every dollar lost to waste or fraud is a dollar that could have funded vital public services. Every corrupt deal that rewards political insiders increases cynicism and makes it harder to build support for ambitious solutions to social problems. But every one of these issues is also an opportunity for activists and politicians to fight back and fix our social contract.

We need to identify and eliminate wasteful government spending and reallocate money from unpopular expenditures like foreign wars to domestic investments like healthcare and education. The true cost of the Iraq War ended up being more than 500,000 lives and $3 trillion, not the $50 billion originally projected by the White House.[107] And the Small Business Administration (SBA) estimates that over $200 billion in COVID-19 relief funds was potentially lost to fraud.[108] It's obvious that we're not maximizing the value of our government spending.

These are real problems. We must fix this waste. But we can't accept the cynics' argument that corruption is inevitable, because this cynicism causes good people to give up on politics and leaves the field open for bad actors to take over. Fixing these problems will not only save our government money; doing so is also essential to unlocking the full potential of Positive Politics. Because when we get more value from our tax dollars, we trust our government to do more for us. This is the idea of state capacity, the ability of a government to effectively provide for its people.

**HOW TO INCREASE OUR STATE CAPACITY**

Fighting to get more value from our government is how we strengthen our social contract. We need more transparency to track which funds are spent directly by our governments versus distributed to contractors and nonprofits to do the work. Both corruption and waste grow in the dark, so we need to expose the flow of our money and find and fix leaks. Positive Politics requires constant work to redirect wasteful spending toward better services for all. But every time we increase state capacity, this starts a positive feedback loop where we earn more public trust, which earns us more resources to increase state capacity again.

These fixes ought to be nonpartisan. Social contract reforms can come from across the political spectrum. In Idaho, Governor Brad Little's "Zero-Based Regulation" order instituted a sunset provision where regulations expire in five years unless renewed by a state agency, which has led to the reduction of thousands of pages of regulations.[109] Governor Tim Walz's "Minnesota Miracle" agenda guaranteed paid family and medical leave, made breakfast and lunch free for all students, and created a new child tax credit, making it easier for families to grow.[110] These state actions give us great examples for national reforms.

## LET'S USE THIS CURRENT PRO-REFORM
## MOOD FOR GOOD

What we need now is a movement of Americans dedicated to fixing this social contract, one reform at a time. The public needs open access to government spending data so everyone can transparently follow where our money goes. Small businesses need open access to government contracts so they can compete with large contractors. And we all need campaign finance reform so more independent people can run for office and win. Many of these changes can be implemented most quickly through executive actions and then made permanent with bills or amendments. Focusing on state and local actions first can also speed up reform.

You don't have to go through politicians to make these changes. Nonprofit organizations like OpenSecrets create more government transparency by tracking campaign finance and lobbying and making it easy for anyone to search this data to follow the money in politics. And rights groups like the American Civil Liberties Union (ACLU) and Electronic Frontier Foundation (EFF) fight court cases and provide legal assistance to defend individual liberties. Check out section 11.2 for more activism ideas you can use now.

All of these solutions will make our government more efficient and accountable and increase our state capacity. Fighting corruption is also an independent nonpartisan issue that we can rally around to build power for our Positive Politics movement. Fixing our social contract will restore faith in democratic institutions and create the conditions for Positive Politics to flourish. This is a meta-solution for the world's biggest problems.

It's time to recruit the next generation of Positive Politicians and get to work passing a new bill of rights that will fix our social contract and bring back the American Dream.

# CHAPTER 11

★ ★ ★

# WHAT'S NEXT?

## 11.1

★

# THE POSITIVE POLITICS ACCELERATOR

*"Ambitious people are rare, so if everyone is mixed together randomly, as they tend to be early in people's lives, then the ambitious ones won't have many ambitious peers. When you take people like this and put them together with other ambitious people, they bloom like dying plants given water."*

—PAUL GRAHAM, *THE ANATOMY OF DETERMINATION*, 2009

### IDEA: CREATE THE Y COMBINATOR FOR POLITICS

On March 11, 2005, Paul Graham and Jessica Livingston had the idea to create an investment firm to invest the first $20,000 into new startups. In those days, raising even $10,000 for a new startup meant personally knowing someone rich, and still usually also required giving up 10 percent or more of your company. This new firm would offer $20,000 for 7 percent on standard transparent terms and also included a three-month "batch" where founders could learn from the partners and their peers. The program now culminates four times a year with a Demo Day, where startups launch to the public and thousands of investors. This accelerator, Y Combinator, has now funded over five thousand companies, with over four hundred startups valued over $100 million and more than ninety valued over $1 billion, and is widely considered the first and best startup accelerator in the world.[111]

### A FEW KEY CHARACTERISTICS MAKE YC SO SUCCESSFUL

1. **Early belief:** YC's partners are all startup founders, and many have gone through the program themselves. Their self-fulfilling belief in startups is something founders and investors can trust.
   - Lesson: We all remember the first person who truly believed in our potential. This is especially true in start-ups and politics, where the journey to success can take a decade or longer.
2. **Trusted network:** YC's founder network is both open (anyone can apply) and exclusive (less than 1 percent acceptance rate). These two factors combine to create an extremely meritocratic community of founders.
   - Lesson: Most powerful political networks today rely on connections between billionaires and the political elite. We will build an open and exclusive network of Positive Politicians who will change the world.
3. **Lead investor:** YC's standard deal increased to $120,000 per startup in 2014 and $500,000 per startup in 2022. This

anchor investment leads to many new YC startups raising millions of dollars just months later at Demo Day.

- Lesson: As with EMILYs List, early money helps raise more money. We will recruit, vet, and train these candidates so they're ready to launch quickly.

4. **True independence:** There were startup incubators before YC. But they all sought to significantly own and control their creations. YC is different—it rides alongside founders on the cap table but lets them lead.

- Lesson: We need to keep this accelerator independent of all parties, factions, and special interests. We support anyone who follows our principles through our accelerator and our community.

A political accelerator that embodies these principles could help launch the careers of thousands of new positive activists and politicians.

## RIGHT NOW, THERE ARE ONLY TWO MAIN PATHS INTO US POLITICS

1. Network and fundraise from the Democratic or Republican establishment.
   - This system tends to promote privileged, ambitious, well-spoken insiders.
2. Make millions of dollars in another career, then self-finance your own races.
   - These politicians are usually more independent, but this path can take decades.

Does it feel like every election is a choice between two bad candidates? If you're mad about candidate quality, focus on candidate recruitment. We don't get the candidates we deserve. We get the candidates we recruit and support—so let's accelerate many more new candidates.

## WE NEED TO CREATE AN ACCELERATED PATH INTO POLITICS FOR FUTURE POSITIVE POLITICIANS

I'm calling this the Positive Politics Accelerator. Here's the plan:

1. Recruit hundreds of future Positive Politicians.
2. Train them to win elections and pass positive-sum bills.
3. Solve the world's biggest problems through politics.

This combines an accelerator program like Y Combinator with a funding model like EMILYs List. Of course, we can't use equity. These will have to be transparent political donations to each candidate. Using EMILYs List's bundling model, we could seed the first $100,000 or more of each Positive Politician's campaign, which could kick-start millions of dollars in fundraising so our candidates could even run for federal elections. Success would mean thousands of Positive Politicians all over the country, and around the world, all fighting for their key issues.

I've had the full YC experience, being accepted in 2014, graduating and raising $1.5 million in 2015, raising another $4 million in 2016, and becoming profitable by 2018. I know how this program changed my life, and I would love to build the Positive Politics version of this accelerator.

One of the most amazing things about YC is the wide range of origin stories. You'll have three teenage founders from India working next to a family of five founders from Missouri—one of their startups working on consumer financial software and the other building a construction equipment network—sitting for dinner weekly with hundreds of other founders from around the world working on hundreds of problems, all motivated by "making something people want." The political version of this network would positively change politics and the world.

The Positive Politics Accelerator will create a new path for elite individuals to start a career in politics. YC proved that "young hackers can start viable companies." Our accelerator will prove that ambitious optimists can win elections and do good.

## WE NEED TO RECRUIT MORE LOCAL LEADERS INTO POLITICS

As the critic Anton Ego said in the movie *Ratatouille*, "The world is often unkind to new talent, new creations. The new needs friends."[112] The same is true in politics. We aim to be the first supporter for thousands of rising political stars.

This means more than just being the first donor and advisor. This means building a network of Positive Politicians who can help each other and work together to pass legislation and build a movement to encourage many more ambitious optimists to get into politics.

Success will mean hundreds of new altruistic politicians, government officials, activists, organizers, intellectuals, influencers, and more, at all levels of politics. It takes less than a thousand good politicians to positively change global politics forever.

This Positive Politics Accelerator is a meta-solution to our political problems because it will recruit many more ambitious optimists like you, who are most motivated by making a positive impact on the world. These new Positive Politicians need friends and advisors, and that's how we aim to serve here.

Check out section 11.2 for my list of the top ten bills that Positive Politicians should focus on first. It frustrates me when political books inspire me to start now but don't give me concrete ways to get involved. This section and the conclusion are focused on specific resources you can use to start with activism and fight for the fundamentals in politics now.

*If you are interested in joining the Positive Politics Accelerator, working for this accelerator, or donating to this accelerator, please visit positivepolitics.org.*

**11.2**

✳

# PASS A NEW BILL OF RIGHTS

*"No society can make a perpetual constitution, or even a perpetual law. The earth belongs always to the living generation."*

—THOMAS JEFFERSON

In a 1789 letter to James Madison, Thomas Jefferson proposed a now radical idea—that the US Constitution and all of its laws be "expressly limited to 19 years only." This would allow every new generation to rule themselves. As Jefferson argued, otherwise, "if...enforced longer, it is an act of force, & not of right."[113] Madison disagreed with the idea of an automatically expiring constitution, believing that nations need fundamental laws. But he did lead the creation of the original

Bill of Rights that same year to guarantee specific personal freedoms.

Madison proposed twelve amendments—ten were ratified in 1791, one was ratified in 1992 (see Chapter 7), and one is still pending. After ratifying ten amendments to the Constitution in two years, America has ratified only seventeen more amendments in the following 234 years. Positive Politicians should bring back the Founding Fathers' spirit of reform and create a new Bill of Rights for our generation.

## WE NEED A NEW PRO-DEMOCRACY MOVEMENT IN AMERICA

*Note: The rest of this chapter will get prescriptive on specific reforms I believe Positive Politicians should pursue now to get wins quickly and think long term. You'll likely not agree with every idea, but this is meant to be a menu for you to use to get started. Feel free to choose your own path.*

When imagining pro-democracy protests, we may picture Tiananmen Square or Tahrir Square rather than Wall Street or the National Mall. But there's a long history of pro-democracy protests in America too. From Occupy Wall Street to the civil rights movement to the Progressive Era of the late nineteenth and early twentieth centuries, Americans have risen up time and time again to fight for more rights and a better government.

We need a new Progressive Era in America to fight corruption, increase transparency, and reallocate the money we're wasting now to improve the fundamentals of economic opportunity. As we discussed in Chapters 5 and 6, fighting for these fundamentals will give more Americans the freedom to succeed. What Americans positively do with that freedom, for themselves, their families, and their communities, will be the lasting return from these investments.

We can save money and change lives at the same time. For example, a single-payer healthcare system would save sixty-eight thousand lives, 1.73 million life years (a quality-of-life metric), and $450 billion every year.[114] And we should redistribute billions of dollars in wasted government spending to social programs like childcare and job training that will help current and future generations live happier, more productive lives. The government is at its best when it provides fundamental services for a lower price than we could get if we all paid individually.

## ONE WAY TO FIX OUR POLITICAL SYSTEM

We can't just run for office. We must fix the political system itself. As we discussed in Chapter 5, Positive Politicians should focus on meta-solutions to our biggest problems. For example, I'm fighting for open government as executive director of the Michigan Campaign Finance Network (MCFN), investigating dark money in politics and publishing research to inform the public and politicians on issues like freedom of information and the influence of corporations and wealthy individuals on our government.

Since the *Citizens United v. FEC* Supreme Court ruling in 2010 barred restrictions on independent expenditures in politics, billionaire spending on federal elections is sixty times higher.[115] Winning US House members spend over $2 million per election, and winning US Senate members spend over $20 million per election.[116] This skews Congress toward the wealthy—over half of all members of Congress are millionaires.[117] We clearly need campaign finance reform. Fighting for political transparency, with the aim of a truly open government, is my contribution to politics now.

Campaign finance reform is a key meta-solution to our political problems because when elections are largely decided by money, establishment insiders cater to their donors more than their constituents. This skews public policy toward regulatory capture and tax cuts for wealthy people and corporations and away from positive-sum solutions for lower- and middle-class Americans. There are many other important issues like this one that you can focus on now.

## MORE FUNDAMENTAL ISSUES TO BE SOLVED

Don't know which issue you want to focus on now? This is the fun part! Search through the major meta-solutions and see which ones spark your energy and might affect you personally. As we discussed in section 6.2, it doesn't matter which issue you choose, and you can always change your mind in a year or two. But find an area where you could happily spend a decade or more working toward a goal and get started now. The following is my ranking of the top ten meta-solutions that you can work on in activism, politics, or government now.

| 1. Equal opportunity | Finally pass the Equal Rights Amendment (ERA) and guarantee equal legal rights for all Americans. |
| --- | --- |
| 2. Open government | Every American has the right to freedom of information from its government and elected officials. |
| 3. Transparent politics | Every citizen has the right to free and fair elections, including equal representation and easy ways to vote. |
| 4. Education access | Every American has the right to access public education from preschool through college. |
| 5. Healthcare access | Every American has the right to access lifesaving medical care, including preventative services. |
| 6. Housing access | America should expand public and private housing programs to ensure that every American can afford housing. |
| 7. Living wage | America should expand public jobs programs to ensure that every American can earn a living wage. |
| 8. Healthy planet | America should lead the world in protecting the environment for current and future generations. |
| 9. Bodily autonomy | Every American has the exclusive right to make decisions about their own bodies. |
| 10. Digital privacy | Every American has the exclusive right to their own data and cannot be tracked without explicit consent. |

## WRITING CAN TURN ACTIVISM INTO POLITICS

Words matter. The very first pro-democracy movement in America was driven by the writings of leaders like Benjamin Franklin and Alexander Hamilton. The Progressive Era was driven by investigative journalists like Ida Tarbell and Upton Sinclair. Tarbell's book about the Standard Oil monopoly led to the creation of the Federal Trade Commission (FTC), and Sinclair's book about the meatpacking industry led to the passage of the 1906 Pure Food and Drug Act.

We need more modern muckrakers. Nonprofit organizations like ProPublica and MCFN are using investigative journalism and data analysis to expose government corruption and corporate fraud. And as technology continues to advance, the potential for using AI and other tools to uncover loopholes in legislation and waste and fraud in government spending could finally allow us to review millions of documents and transactions to find suspicious patterns for journalists and the public to pursue. Building these government transparency tools is a key meta-solution to making politics more positive.

**PICK YOUR ISSUES AND FOCUS ON THEM FULLY**

*Positive Politics* is a playbook, not a rulebook. You can use these political strategies to fight for any issues you want to solve. What's most important is that you use the Positive Politics principles to do the work and spread the word. I'm excited to work with you in the world of politics soon. Get started now!

# CONCLUSION

*"If you're always trying to be normal, you will never know how amazing you can be."*

—MAYA ANGELOU

## "SÍ, SE PUEDE"

Dolores Huerta was born in 1930 in New Mexico to a coal miner father who became a union leader and state representative and a mother who became an entrepreneur. Huerta became a teacher and then an organizer, focusing on labor rights and co-founding the Agricultural Workers Association (AWA) and the National Farm Workers Association (NFWA).

Starting in 1965, Huerta led five years of strikes and boycotts against grape growers in Delano, California, to fight the exploitation of farmworkers. This led to new contracts, safety rules, and a health fund for the workers by 1970 and the first law providing collective bargaining rights to farmworkers in California in 1975. Huerta co-led the negotiating and lobbying for these wins.

The motto Huerta created in 1972, "Sí, se puede," which literally translates to "Yes, it can be done," also inspired President Barack Obama's famous 2008 campaign slogan "Yes, we can." Dolores Huerta still marches and is active in politics at over ninety-five years old. She also has eleven children and many grand- and great-grandchildren. That's a full life! Huerta's legacy was shaped by her political activism—profoundly meaningful work that made the world a better place. Like Huerta, you too can create meaning, purpose, and a powerful legacy by positively getting into politics now.

Watch *Dolores* (2017), a PBS documentary directed by Peter Bratt, to see the importance of collective action and the power of starting with local activism.

## 1. POSITIVITY IS ALREADY AN IMPORTANT PART OF OUR POLITICS

Being positive won't guarantee you'll win 100 percent of your elections. No political playbook can honestly promise that. But just like the game theory of the prisoner's dilemma proves that being nice first is a winning strategy, even if you initially lose once or twice, Positive Politics maximizes your long-term chances of success, even if it opens you up to attacks. Being nice, flexible, provokable, and predictable makes it easy for politicians to cooperate with you and for the public to trust you. These political strategies are tried-and-true methods that have worked for centuries in America and around the world.

This book highlights many different politicians and activists, past and present, who already exemplify the Positive Politics principles, even if they call their system by a different name. This includes people working outside the system, like the civil rights leaders and nonprofit founders who organize people and money toward positive ends. Let's keep celebrating people who make Positive Politics possible.

We should also commend those inside our government quietly making positive change, like the recipients of Samuel J. Heyman Service to America Medals, also known as "the Sammies," celebrating excellence in American federal service. Too much media attention today is focused on politicians attacking each other and accusing the other party of destroying our country. To counter this negativity, we need to focus our time and energy to spotlight the people taking positive action and making political progress now.

## 2. POLITICS SOLVES OUR BIGGEST PROBLEMS

Our world could be so much better if everyone reading this book immediately got into politics. Politics is both the largest and oldest industry in the world. If you want to make the greatest positive impact, you have to get into politics. It's easy to get frustrated by the corruption and waste in our current government. But the truth is that most government workers are nonpartisan service workers doing their best to help people. If you see something wrong, fix it. Politics is the best way to solve these major problems.

Governments get a lot of criticism, but they quietly do massive good. Governments don't just run military and social programs; they're responsible for many of our largest scientific and technological breakthroughs. Businesses can make billion-dollar investments, but only governments can make trillion-dollar investments. Businesses think in quarters and years; governments think in decades and centuries. We all need these fundamental government investments to be maximally successful. Help make these investments for future generations.

### 3. THIS IS THE PERFECT TIME FOR POSITIVE POLITICS

Don't wait until you're already rich and successful in another field to get active in politics. Make politics your job, your passion, and your career now. Instead of focusing on money now and meaning later, do both now—you can start with activism while you're in your first career. Or better yet, make politics your full-time job. Both of these things changed my life and can change your life too if you take the leap.

Negativity may be winning now, but there's a long history and future of positivity in politics. The pendulum is always swinging in politics, and we're due for another period of prosocial positivity like the early Progressive Era of the turn of the previous century or the civil rights movement of the 1960s. More importantly, our world is getting richer in many ways, including in terms of access to cheaper and cleaner technology and energy. New scientific advances in the coming decades will bring this abundance to food, water, and medicine, making it easier to provide government services to all. Positive Politics will thrive in these conditions.

## 4. POLITICS WILL MAKE YOUR LIFE MORE MEANINGFUL

I bet you're already successful in your life. You could stay on your current path and be comfortable, accumulating wealth for yourself and your family. Or you could do something bigger and change the course of history. Which will you choose? If you pick politics, your whole life will become bigger.

You are capable of so much more than getting rich. Impact is measured in lives changed, not money earned. Rise to the challenge of public service. Spend a few years using all of your energy and passion to fight for your favorite causes. You're so close to a new, more exciting life. Get into politics now!

Your skills are valuable and needed in politics. I've helped many successful professionals get more active in politics, from volunteering for campaigns to advocating for new legislation to growing new nonprofits. Smart people often remain stuck in their first careers long after these careers have made them safe and successful. Politics forces us to think beyond ourselves, quit being critics, and get in the arena. I love seeing people become positively transformed by politics—you can be next.

## 5. POSITIVE POLITICS WON'T JUST HAPPEN—WE NEED TO FIGHT FOR IT

Politics—or more precisely, arguing about politics—feels like everyone's side job today. So it may seem odd that I'm suggesting even more political participation. But the hard truth is that social media "debates" don't do much to fix politics. You have to stop screaming from the stands and get in the game. Start by focusing on the fundamentals, like education, healthcare, jobs, housing, and transparency to provide more economic opportunity to all and earn more trust for governments. This will give all Americans more freedom to succeed.

We need a Positive Politics movement full of ambitious optimists like you, who are ready to fight to change the world. Political movements don't just happen naturally. They're led by people who decided to take direct action. It's easy to be cynical about politics and worry about the Bad Future. But we have the power to create the Good Future. Let's use this power. By creating meta-solutions to our fundamental problems, Positive Politicians can reclaim the American Dream and make our future better for all.

## 6. ACTIVISM IS YOUR GATEWAY INTO POLITICS

If you're angry about the state of politics now, channel your anger and frustration into activism. By starting with activism, you can start influencing politics now and learn how the system works so you'll be ready when you want to run for politics. A great way to get stuff done in politics is to focus on a specific issue and turn your ideas into bills. You don't need any specific political experience to get started in activism. Once you've built a reputation for getting good activism work done, use that power to get into politics.

Meta-solutions are how to make the most impact in activism. Think campaign finance reform: if we fight unlimited dark money in politics, we could have far fewer negative ads polluting our politics and more space for new ambitious optimists to run for office. Focus on the fundamentals when finding your issues to help give Americans the freedom to succeed. Imagine millions of more people with the time and energy to create a better future for themselves, their families, and their communities. Empowering these people is a meta-solution for the world that will help make Positive Politics possible for future generations too.

## 7. FOCUS ON ACTIONS OVER WORDS TO GET STUFF DONE

Direct political action is available to anyone at any time. From making a one-minute phone call to your congressman to tell them how to vote on your favorite bill to embarking on a decade-plus journey to build your own political nonprofit, there is always something you can do to positively influence your government. You don't have to be a politician to take these actions. Writing essays and bills, organizing activists and volunteers, and calling and lobbying legislators are all outsider paths to getting things done in activism. Start taking direct political action now.

A core skill in activism and politics is turning your ideas into bills. Activism solves this problem by building popular support for just and moral causes. Politics takes these ideas over the finish line once they're popular by building coalitions and organizing majority support in legislatures. The journey from bill to law is important, but going from idea to bill is always necessary first. Becoming proficient at the idea-to-law pipeline is critical to being a successful Positive Politician.

## 8. EARN POLITICAL POWER THAT YOU CAN USE TO ORGANIZE COLLECTIVE ACTION

Politics works best when you make big promises and then deliver. This builds public trust and confidence in your abilities. As the Positive Politics principles "take action" and "get wins quickly" recommend, focusing on issues over attacks and getting things done are key to succeeding in politics.

Once you've built a positive record of political wins, you'll earn the right to take bigger and bolder actions. This includes running for higher office and convincing larger branches of government to positively change. Study the insider and outsider routes taken by famous activists and politicians throughout history and see what paths are open to you now. It doesn't matter how you start—just get started!

Organizing collective action is how to scale up activism and politics. The skills needed to succeed here are very similar to those needed in startups. You need to be able to understand marketing, communications, strategy, finance, operations, legal, and more, all while building great teams to do this work. The good news is that once you build these political power structures, you can use them for decades.

## 9. WINNING ELECTIONS IS MORE ABOUT YOUR MESSAGE THAN MONEY

The best long-term strategy in political communications is to go directly to voters with a positive vision and agenda. Franklin Roosevelt famously broadcast his fireside chats over the radio to directly reach the public and was also the first president to speak on television. Barack Obama's 2008 presidential campaign was the first to use social media to directly reach voters, building a movement around a "Hope and Change" message that could be easily shared through photos and videos. And as Alexandria Ocasio-Cortez said before her first primary win, "You can't really beat big money with more money. You have to beat them with a totally different game."[118] AOC was outraised over ten to one by her incumbent opponent in that race but still won by 15 percent. Positive Politicians who shape their messages to fit modern media will need less money to win elections.

Following the Positive Politics principles maximizes your expected impact regardless of the races you run or organizations you lead. You can focus on activism for your whole life and still change laws and lives like Dolores Huerta. Or you can transition from activism to politics like John Lewis and lead the government from within. Our principles—be nice, take action, get wins quickly, think long term, go direct, and be independent—work at any level inside or outside politics. What's most important is what you do once you win.

## 10. USE POSITIVE POLITICS TO CHANGE THE WORLD

It's called public service for a reason. Governments serve people. Being a great public servant means finding out what the people want and then figuring out how to efficiently deliver it to them. Use the power of your political voice to organize direct action and inspire more ambitious optimists to get into politics. The sum of all of these actions is Positive Politics.

The ultimate goal of Positive Politics is to help people make the world a better place. You have an amazing opportunity to take what you've learned in this book and put it into action in politics. I know you will be positively transformed the first time one of your direct actions results in political change. Keep going—this is the best part!

## GET INTO POLITICS NOW!

If you need one last piece of encouragement that going into politics and doing good is the right path for you, remember what Martin Luther King Jr. once said: "This hour in history needs a dedicated circle of transformed nonconformists... The saving of our world from pending doom will come, not through the complacent adjustment of a conforming majority, but through the creative maladjustment of a dedicated minority."[119] We are in that hour of history again. It's our time. Let's start this movement!

*If you want to work with me personally, go to positivepolitics.org to see our latest events and sign up for our Positive Politics Accelerator!*

# ACKNOWLEDGMENTS

**THIS BOOK IS FOR ALL THE FUTURE ACTIVISTS AND POLITICIANS WHO WILL SAVE THE WORLD!**

Especially my kids, Kai, Ajay, and Maya, my three happy warriors. I love seeing your faces light up when you learn something new. Your smiles and hugs light up my whole world. Daddy loves you and always believes in you! Please go fight for Positive Politics!

Thank you to my three parents, Shri, Shashi, and Shamal. Dad, everyone knows your successes, but what makes you special to me is that you kept our family together through our hardest moments. So many families fall apart after losses, but you got stronger, and that's why we're all here. Mom, you're truly an angel; you made our lives complete again. Thank you for always being my biggest cheerleader. You always know when I need extra support. And to Mama, I will always love you and carry you with me. We miss you!

Thank you to my wife, Shoua, who has been with me for over fifteen years while I've chased huge dreams! I still remember the first time we met in college; it felt like the rest of the world vanished and the only thing that mattered was the power of our connection. Sometimes we still feel like those kids, which is a good thing! But I wouldn't trade the family and life we've created together for anything.

Thank you to my brother, Samir, who always finds time for us to talk. Our childhood adventures sparked my curiosity and imagination, and our backyard sports marathons made us both stronger. And to my high school teammates, college crew, and hockey buddies, who always bust my chops and push me to be better. Y'all always know when I need to be humbled!

Thank you to my publisher, Scribe Media, especially my writing coach, Greta Myers, who helped me take this book from good to great, and my publishing manager, Jamie Cappelletti, who helped make this book real! Thank you to Rachael Brandenburg for designing the book covers, Dave Jarecki for editing the final manuscript, Caroline Hough and Cindy Angelini for proofreading, and Ami Hendrickson for copywriting. And thank you to Scribe CEO Eric Jorgenson for pushing me to write this book!

Thank you to my co-founders, Shri, Helton, and Rafael. The days and nights we spent struggling to succeed are now some of my fondest memories. Thanks for teaching me the value of complete trust and the power of true professionalism.

And thank you to the angels and advisors who invested in me early, like Scott Case, Halle Tecco, Mark Cuban, Paul Graham, Mike Maples, Ann Miura-Ko, and hundreds of crowdfunders. We've built something great together, and that story's not over yet!

You all helped me get here!

# NOTES

1     Becky Little, "How a Petty Snub Led to Clinton's Government Shutdown—and the Lewinsky Affair," History, last updated August 19, 2025, https://www.history.com/articles/bill-clinton-government-shutdown-lewinsky-affair.

2     "User Clip: Clinton Addresses Federal Government Shutdown 11/14/1995," C-SPAN, November 14, 1995, https://www.c-span.org/clip/white-house-event/user-clip-clinton-addresses-federal-government-shutdown-11-14-1995/4621051.

3     *The Clinton Affair*, season 1, episode 2, "The Blue Pass," directed by Blair Foster, November 18, 2018, Jigsaw Productions, https://www.aetv.com/shows/the-clinton-affair/season-1/episode-2.

4     McKay Coppins, "The Man Who Broke Politics," *The Atlantic*, last updated October 17, 2018, https://www.theatlantic.com/magazine/archive/2018/11/newt-gingrich-says-youre-welcome/570832/.

5     "As Partisan Hostility Grows, Signs of Frustration with the Two-Party System," Pew Research Center, August 9, 2022, https://www.pewresearch.org/politics/2022/08/09/as-partisan-hostility-grows-signs-of-frustration-with-the-two-party-system/.

6     Robert McNeely, "President Clinton and Newt Gingrich in Congressional budget meeting," National Archives Catalog, December 30, 1995, https://catalog.archives.gov/id/183373990.

7     Steven M. Gillon, *The Pact: Bill Clinton, Newt Gingrich, and the Rivalry That Defined a Generation* (Oxford University Press, 2008).

8     "Public Trust in Government: 1958–2024," Pew Research Center, June 24, 2024, https://www.pewresearch.org/politics/2024/06/24/public-trust-in-government-1958-2024/.

9   Tim Alberta, "'The Woman in Michigan' Goes National," Politico, April 9, 2020, https://www.politico.com/news/magazine/2020/04/09/gretchen-whitmer-governor-michigan-profile-2020-coronavirus-biden-vp-177791.

10  Arnold Schwarzenegger, "Second Inaugural Address," The Governors' Gallery, January 5, 2007, https://governors.library.ca.gov/addresses/38-schwarzenegger02.html.

11  Jeff Jackson, "The Angriest Voices in Congress Are Mostly Faking," Quick Update (Substack), April 18, 2023, https://jeffjacksonnc.substack.com/p/the-angriest-voices-in-congress-are.

12  Jackson, "Angriest Voices."

13  James Tobin, "The Prisoner's Dilemma," University of Michigan Heritage Project, accessed August 28, 2025, https://heritage.umich.edu/stories/the-prisoners-dilemma/.

14  Nobel Prize Outreach, news release, October 11, 1994, https://www.nobelprize.org/prizes/economic-sciences/1994/press-release/.

15  Rich Gorecki, "Ronald Reagan and Tip O'Neill: A Real-Life Friendship," Boston College, August 28, 2023, https://www.bc.edu/bc-web/centers/church21/publications/c21-resources/c21-resources-articles/Ronald-Reagan-and-Tip-O-Neill--A-Real-life-Friendship.html.

16  "McCain Counters Obama 'Arab' Question," October 11, 2008, posted by Associated Press, YouTube, https://www.youtube.com/watch?v=jrnRU30cIH4.

17  Charles J. Stewart, Craig A. Smith, and Robert E. Denton, Persuasion and Social Movements (Waveland Press, 1994).

18  Harriet I. Flower, Roman Republics (Princeton University Press, 2011).

19  Kathryn Selig Brown, "Life of the Buddha," The Metropolitan Museum of Art, October 1, 2003, https://www.metmuseum.org/essays/life-of-the-buddha; Taylor Branch, Parting the Waters: America in the King Years, 1954–63 (Simon & Schuster, 1989); Rob Sellers, "Jesus and Gandhi: A Study in Commonalities," Christian Ethics Today, April 2, 2022, https://christianethicstoday.com/wp/jesus-and-gandhi-a-study-in-commonalities/.

20  Plato, "The Republic", trans. Allan Bloom, 2nd ed. (New York: Basic Books, 1991), 347c, p. 25.

21  "User Clip: Congress Spontaneous Sings God Bless America," C-SPAN, September 11, 2001, https://www.c-span.org/clip/news-conference/user-clip-congress-spontaneous-sings-god-bless-america-9-11-01/4816002.

22  C-SPAN, "Congress Sings."

23  Joseph E. Aldy et al., "Looking Back at 50 Years of the Clean Air Act of 1970," Resources, June 15, 2020, https://www.resources.org/archives/looking-back-50-years-clean-air-act-1970/.

24  Environmental Protection Agency, "Our Nation's Air - Trends Through 2023," August 16, 2024, https://gispub.epa.gov/air/trendsreport/2024/.

25  Amy West, "Congress Is Busy with Under-the-Radar Bipartisan Legislation," Fulcrum, April 16, 2024, https://thefulcrum.us/governance-legislation/bipartisan-legislation.

26  Jacob Fabina et al., "School Enrollment in the United States: 2021," US Census Bureau, June 2023, https://www.census.gov/content/dam/Census/library/publications/2023/acs/acs-55.pdf.

27  Fabina et. al., "School Enrollment."

28  "Who Is Receiving Social Safety Net Benefits?" US Census Bureau, July 10, 2024, https://www.census.gov/library/visualizations/interactive/social-safety-net-benefits.html.

29  "A Growing Number of Governments Hope to Clone America's DARPA," *The Economist*, June 3, 2021, https://www.economist.com/science-and-technology/2021/06/03/a-growing-number-of-governments-hope-to-clone-americas-darpa.

30  Elisa Muyl and Anthony Lydgate, "How Trump Killed Cancer Research," *Wired*, July 21, 2025, https://www.wired.com/story/how-trump-killed-cancer-research/.

31  Keith Perine, "The Early Adopter—Al Gore and the Internet—Government Activity," *The Industry Standard*, October 23, 2000, https://archive.is/l9zK.

32  Al Gore, "The Technology Challenge: How Can America Spark Private Innovation?," speech, University of Pennsylvania, February 14, 1996, Philadelphia, PA, https://homes.cs.washington.edu/~lazowska/faculty.lecture/innovation/gore.html.

33  Martin Beraja et al., "Government as Venture Capitalists in AI," Working Paper No. 32701 (National Bureau of Economic Research, July 2024), https://www.nber.org/papers/w32701.

34  Drew DeSilver, "Age and Generation in the 119th Congress: Somewhat Younger, with Fewer Boomers and More Gen Xers," Pew Research Center, January 16, 2025, https://www.pewresearch.org/short-reads/2025/01/16/age-and-generation-in-the-119th-congress-somewhat-younger-with-fewer-boomers-and-more-gen-xers/.

35  DeSilver, "Age and Generation."

36  Christopher Wlezien, "The Public as Thermostat: Dynamics of Preferences for Spending," *American Journal of Political Science* 39, no. 4 (1995): 981–1000, https://doi.org/10.2307/2111666.

37  James Stimson, "Data," The University of North Carolina at Chapel Hill, accessed September 17, 2025, https://stimson.web.unc.edu/data/.

38  Stimson, "Data."

39  Martin Hilbert, "Digital Technology and Social Change: The Digital Transformation of Society from a Historical Perspective," *Dialogues in Clinical Neuroscience* 22, no. 2 (2022): 189–94, https://doi.org/10.31887/DCNS.2020.22.2/mhilbert.

40  Ed Gordon, "The Montgomery Bus Boycott, 50 Years Later," NPR, December 1, 2005, https://www.npr.org/2005/12/01/5033971/the-montgomery-bus-boycott-50-years-later.

41  "Congressman John R. Lewis," Academy of Achievement, last revised April 5, 2022, https://achievement.org/achiever/congressman-john-r-lewis/.

42  "Jennifer E. Manning, Membership of the 118th Congress: A Profile," Library of Congress, December 12, 2024, https://www.congress.gov/crs-product/R47470.

43  Alexander Hamilton, "To the Royal Danish American Gazette" *The Royal Danish American Gazette* (St. Croix), September 6, 1772, https://founders.archives.gov/documents/Hamilton/01-01-02-0042.

44  *Chicago Tribune*, January 17, 1900, 14, https://www.newspapers.com/article/chicago-tribune/84907355/.

45  Peter Economy, "Steve Jobs and His Remarkable Simple Secret of Life," *Inc.*, June 18, 2015, https://www.inc.com/peter-economy/steve-jobs-on-the-1-remarkably-simple-secret-of-life.html.

46  William Gibson, "The Science in Science Fiction," interview by Brooke Gladstone, *Talk of the Nation*, October 22, 2018, https://www.npr.org/2018/10/22/1067220/the-science-in-science-fiction.

47  Libby Stanford, "Which States Offer Universal Pre-K? It's More Complicated Than You Might Think," EducationWeek, January 25, 2023, https://www.edweek.org/teaching-learning/which-states-offer-universal-pre-k-its-more-complicated-than-you-might-think/2023/01.

48   "The Faircloth Amendment Blocks the Construction of Affordable Housing: It Should Be Repealed," Center for Economic and Policy Research, December 11, 2024, https://cepr.net/publications/the-faircloth-amendment-blocks-the-construction-of-affordable-housing-it-should-be-repealed/.

49   Xinhua, "China Accelerates Construction of Government-Subsidized Rental Housing Projects," *China Daily*, September 14, 2023, https://www.chinadaily.com.cn/a/202309/14/WS65026953a310d2dce4bb5aa4.html.

50   Stephen Dover and Tracy Chen, hosts, *Talking Markets*, podcast, "A Tale of Two Real Estate Markets: US and China," January 4, 2022, https://www.franklintempleton.com/insights/podcasts/a-tale-of-two-real-estate-markets-us-and-china.

51   Frank Newport, "Exploring Americans' Satisfaction with Their Personal Lives," Gallup, February 16, 2024, https://news.gallup.com/opinion/polling-matters/610742/exploring-americans-satisfaction-personal-lives.aspx.

52   Newport, "Exploring Americans' Satisfaction."

53   Ben Prentice, "WTF Happened in 1971?," accessed November 25, 2024, https://wtfhappenedin1971.com/.

54   Emmanuel Saez, "Striking it Richer: The Evolution of Top Incomes in the United States," UC Berkeley, February 2020, https://eml.berkeley.edu/~saez/saez-UStopincomes-2018.pdf.

55   Tax Policy Center, "Historical Highest Marginal Income Tax Rates," May 11, 2023, https://taxpolicycenter.org/statistics/historical-highest-marginal-income-tax-rates.

56   John F. Kennedy Jr., "Address at Rice University on the Nation's Space Effort," September 12, 1962, John F. Kennedy Presidential Library and Museum, transcript and audio, https://www.jfklibrary.org/learn/about-jfk/historic-speeches/address-at-rice-university-on-the-nations-space-effort.

57   Riley Beggin, "One Woman's Facebook Post Leads to Michigan Vote Against Gerrymandering," Bridge Michigan, November 7, 2018, https://bridgemi.com/michigan-government/one-womans-facebook-post-leads-michigan-vote-against-gerrymandering/.

58   "State Legislative Update: Independent Citizen-Redistricting Commissions," American Academy of Arts & Sciences, April 29, 2025, https://www.amacad.org/news/state-legislative-update-independent-citizen-redistricting-commissions.

59   Craig Mauger, "Michigan Campaign Will Seek to Ban Political Giving by Utilities, State Contractors," *The Detroit News*, June 30, 2025, https://www.detroitnews.com/story/news/politics/2025/06/30/michigan-campaign-seeks-ban-political-giving-utilities-contractors-transparency-voters/84388822007/.

60   "Levels of Government: Federal, State, Local," Pew Research Center, June 6, 2022, https://www.pewresearch.org/politics/2022/06/06/levels-of-government-federal-state-local/.

61   Anna Massoglia, "Dark Money Hit a Record High of $1.9 Billion in 2024 Federal Races," Brennan Center for Justice, May 7, 2025, https://www.brennancenter.org/our-work/research-reports/dark-money-hit-record-high-19-billion-2024-federal-races.

62   Conor Dougherty, "The 'Georgists' Are Out There, and They Want to Tax Your Land," *The New York Times*, November 12, 2023, https://www.nytimes.com/2023/11/12/business/georgism-land-tax-housing.html.

63   "Economic Rent," Henry George Foundation, accessed August 28, 2025, https://henrygeorgefoundation.org/economic-justice/economic-rent.

64   Editors of Encyclopaedia Britannica, "Biography of Henry George," Britannica, accessed June 30, 2025, https://www.britannica.com/money/Henry-George.

65  Andrew Daniller, "Americans See a Role for the Federal Government in Many Domains, but Some Large Partisan Divisions Persist," Pew Research Center, May 6, 2025, https://www.pewresearch.org/short-reads/2025/05/06/americans-see-a-role-for-the-federal-government-in-many-domains-but-some-large-partisan-divisions-persist/.

66  Rachel White, "The 'C' That Changed the Constitution," *Life & Letters*, January 11, 2018. https://lifeandletters.la.utexas.edu/2018/01/the-c-that-changed-the-constitution/.

67  White, "The 'C.'"

68  Paul Kiel, "Blogosphere Unites in Pursuit of Masked Senator," *TPMmuckraker* (blog) August 28, 2006, https://web.archive.org/web/20060830224720/http://www.tpmmuckraker.com/archives/001428.php.

69  "Doris 'Granny D' Haddock," New Hampshire Radical History, May 10, 2021, https://www.nhradicalhistory.org/story/doris-granny-d-haddock/.

70  "Feb. 29, 2000: 'Granny D' Completes Walk for Campaign Finance Reform," Zinn Education Project, accessed May 29, 2025, https://www.zinnedproject.org/news/tdih/granny-d-completes-walk.

71  Liz Iacobucci, "Remembering 'Granny D'—Her Statement on May 24, 2000," Open Democracy, May 24, 2017, https://www.opendemocracynh.org/granny_d_court_statement.

72  Tom Williams, *90-Year-Old Political Activist Doris 'Granny D' Haddock Speaking at a Podium Outside the U.S. Capitol After Her Walk from Los Angeles to Washington, D.C. in Support of Campaign Finance Reform*, February 29, 2000, photograph, Library of Congress, https://www.loc.gov/resource/ppmsca.38894/.

73  New Hampshire Radical History, "Doris 'Granny D' Haddock."

74  Megan Brenan, "Same-Sex Relations, Marriage Still Supported by Most in U.S.," Gallup, June 24, 2024, https://news.gallup.com/poll/646202/sex-relations-marriage-supported.aspx.

75  "LGBTQ+ Rights," Gallup, accessed January 19, 2024, https://news.gallup.com/poll/1651/gay-lesbian-rights.aspx.

76  Derek Robertson, "How an Obscure Conservative Theory Became the Trump Era's Go-To Nerd Phrase," Politico, February 25, 2018, https://www.politico.com/magazine/story/2018/02/25/overton-window-explained-definition-meaning-217010/.

77  Robertson, "Obscure Conservative Theory."

78  Becky Bowers, "President Barack Obama's Shifting Stance on Gay Marriage," PolitiFact, May 11, 2012, https://www.politifact.com/factchecks/2012/may/11/barack-obama/president-barack-obamas-shift-gay-marriage/.

79  Lydia Saad, "Surge in U.S. Concern About Immigration Has Abated," Gallup, July 11, 2025, https://news.gallup.com/poll/692522/surge-concern-immigration-abated.aspx.

80  Saad, "Surge in U.S. Concern."

81  John Gramlich, "What the Data Says About Crime in the U.S.," Pew Research Center, April 24, 2024, https://www.pewresearch.org/short-reads/2024/04/24/what-the-data-says-about-crime-in-the-us/.

82  Gramlich, "Crime in the U.S."

83  Admin, "Ban on Stock Trading for Members of Congress Favored by Overwhelming Bipartisan Majority," University of Maryland Program for Public Consultation, July 19, 2023, https://publicconsultation.org/united-states/stock-trading-by-members-of-congress/.

84  Laurel Harbridge-Yong et al., "The Bipartisan Path to Effective Lawmaking," *The Journal of Politics* 85, no. 3 (2023): 1048–63, https://doi.org/10.1086/723805.

85  "Top Self-Funding Candidates, 2023–2024," OpenSecrets, accessed August 28, 2025, https://www.opensecrets.org/elections-overview/top-self-funders.

86  Alexander Sammon, "AOC Should Have Won This Fight," *Slate*, December 17, 2024, https://slate.com/news-and-politics/2024/12/pelosi-aoc-democrats-house-oversight-trump.html.

87  Liz Halloran, "Mother of Women's PACs Seeks Younger Supporters," NPR, April 29, 2010, https://www.npr.org/2010/04/29/126393558/mother-of-womens-pacs-seeks-younger-supporters.

88  "Women We've Helped Elect," EMILYs List, last updated July 2025, https://emilyslist.org/candidates/.

89  Molly E. Reynolds and Naomi Maehr, "Vital Statistics on Congress," Brookings Institution, November 4, 2024, https://www.brookings.edu/articles/vital-statistics-on-congress/.

90  Halloran, "Mother of Women's PACs."

91  "Lobbying Data Summary," OpenSecrets, accessed June 30, 2025, https://www.opensecrets.org/federal-lobbying.

92  "Fighting Special Interest Lobbyist Power over Public Policy," Center for American Progress, September 27, 2017, https://www.americanprogress.org/article/fighting-special-interest-lobbyist-power-public-policy/.

93  "Milwaukee Sewer Socialism," Wisconsin Historical Society, accessed June 30, 2025, https://www.wisconsinhistory.org/Records/Article/CS428.

94  "The Long History of the Phrase 'Civil Rights,'" Merriam-Webster, accessed August 28, 2025, https://www.merriam-webster.com/wordplay/civil-rights.

95  "The Senate Passes the Thirteenth Amendment," Senate.gov, accessed August 28, 2025, https://www.senate.gov/about/origins-foundations/senate-and-constitution/senate-passes-the-thirteenth-amendment.htm.

96  Quintus Tullius Cicero, *How to Win an Election*, trans. Philip Freeman (Princeton University Press, 2012), 61.

97  Cicero, *How to Win an Election*, 79.

98  Lindsay M. Chervinsky, "Andrew Jackson's Cabinet," The White House Historical Association, accessed May 8, 2025, https://www.whitehousehistory.org/andrew-jacksons-cabinet.

99  Barnett M. Clinedinst, *President Roosevelt and His Tennis Cabinet*, 1909, photograph, Library of Congress, https://www.loc.gov/resource/ppmsca.37294/.

100 Philip A. Wallach and Nicholas W. Zeppos, "A Look at Spending in the House of Representatives," Brookings Institution, September 20, 2016, https://www.brookings.edu/articles/a-look-at-spending-in-the-house-of-representatives/.

101 Kitty Eisele, "Presidential Campaign Debt Can Linger for Decades," NPR, July 5, 2011, https://www.npr.org/2011/07/05/137615746/presidential-campaign-debt-can-linger-for-decades.

102 Aaron Schein et al., "A Digital Field Experiment Reveals Large Effects of Friend-to-Friend Texting on Voter Turnout," SSRN, October 7, 2020, https://doi.org/10.2139/ssrn.3696179.

103 "Ozone Layer on Track to Recovery: Success Story Should Encourage Action on Climate," United Nations Environment Programme, September 10, 2014, https://web.archive.org/web/20140913031932/http://www.unep.org/newscentre/default.aspx?DocumentID=2796&ArticleID=10978&l=en.

104 Gramlich, "Crime in the U.S."

105  Justin McCarthy, "More Americans Say Crime Is Rising in U.S," Gallup, October 22, 2015, https://news. gallup.com/poll/186308/americans-say-crime-rising.aspx.

106  "Majorities View Local, State, and Federal Taxes as Too High and Delivering Too Little Value for People like Them," NORC at the University of Chicago, January 28, 2024, https://apnorc.org/projects/ majorities-view-local-state-and-federal-taxes-as-too-high-and-delivering-too-little-value-for-people-like-them/.

107  Joseph E. Stiglitz and Linda Bilmes, *The Three Trillion Dollar War* (W. W. Norton, 2008).

108  *COVID-19 Pandemic EIDL and PPP Loan Fraud Landscape* (Small Business Administration, 2023), https://www.sba.gov/document/report-23-09-covid-19-pandemic-eidl-ppp-loan-fraud-landscape.

109  Alex Adams, "Zero-Based Regulation: A Step-by-Step Guide for States," Manhattan Institute, July 18, 2024, https://manhattan.institute/article/zero-based-regulation-a-step-by-step-guide-for-states.

110  Sulma Arias and Analilia Mejia, "Democrats Must Go Big; the Minnesota Miracle Shows Them How," Common Dreams, August 21, 2024, https://www.commondreams.org/opinion/minnesota-miracle.

111  "Resources for Investors," Y Combinator, accessed April 23, 2025, https://www.ycombinator.com/ investors.

112  *Ratatouille*, directed by Brad Bird (Buena Vista Pictures, 2007).

113  Thomas Jefferson, letter to James Madison, September 6, 1789, National Archives, https://founders. archives.gov/documents/Madison/01-12-02-0248.

114  Alison P. Galvani et al., "Improving the Prognosis of Healthcare in the United States," *Lancet* 395, no. 10223 (2020): 524–33, https://doi.org/10.1016/S0140-6736(19)33019-3.

115  "Billionaire Clans Spend Nearly $2 Billion on 2024 Elections," Americans for Tax Fairness, October 29, 2024, https://americansfortaxfairness.org/billionaire-clans-spend-nearly-2-billion-2024-elections/.

116  "Election Trends," OpenSecrets, accessed November 14, 2024, https://www.opensecrets.org/ elections-overview/election-trends.

117  Karl Evers-Hillstrom, "Majority of Lawmakers in 116th Congress Are Millionaires," OpenSecrets, April 23, 2020, https://www.opensecrets.org/news/2020/04/majority-of-lawmakers-millionaires/.

118  Aída Chávez and Ryan Grim, "A Primary Against the Machine: A Bronx Activist Looks to Dethrone Joseph Crowley, the King of Queens," The Intercept, May 22, 2018, https://theintercept. com/2018/05/22/joseph-crowley-alexandra-ocasio-cortez-new-york-primary/.

119  Martin Luther King Jr., *Strength to Love* (Pocket Books, 1964), 16-17.

www.ingramcontent.com/pod-product-compliance
Lightning Source LLC
Chambersburg PA
CBHW031121020426
42333CB00012B/183